Clean Keto

Vegan Recipes for the Good Life

Staci Holweger

Copyright © 2018 Staci Holweger

All rights reserved. No part of this book may be used or reproduced in any manner without written permission except in the case of brief quotations embodied in critical articles and reviews.

For information contact:

Suncoast Digital Press Publishers,
PO Box 50492, Sarasota,
Florida, 34232.

Printed in the United States of America

ISBN 978-1-939237-64-4

FIRST EDITION

All photographs of recipe dishes are taken by the author, Staci Holweger.

PREFACE

The inspiration for this cookbook came from my daughter, Taylor. Four years ago, we were journaling one day and she had written that I should go vegan. Now, at this point in my journey, I had already given up gluten, dairy, and sugar, and had recently decided that I was no longer going to eat any meat or any animal products besides seafood. I was enjoying my salmon and scallops daily, along with lots of veggies—so that day when she told me to go completely vegan, I didn't see it as an option or possibility. But I knew that Taylor was wise beyond her years and had some sort of insight into my life that I did not. I decided to change to veganism, a type of vegetarian diet that excludes meat, eggs, dairy products and all other animal-derived ingredients. "Vegan" refers to either a person who follows this way of eating or to the diet itself.

I didn't realize until recently when I was talking to my son about being vegan that Taylor had also written in her journal that day the word "cookbook." My son asked me why I had decided to become a vegan, so I pulled out his sister's journal and shared with him about the time that she told me to give up salmon and to go vegan. I told him I felt something was guiding her to say that to me and I thought I should give it a try…what did I have to lose? As I skimmed the journal pages to share the conversation with my son, I stopped and caught my breath. The word "cookbook" jumped out at me. I had not remembered that as part of what Taylor journaled that day, even though I always assist her in writing by supporting her wrist, so I should have noticed.

Let me share a bit of her story with you. When Taylor was four, she was misdiagnosed with several different types of cancers and we ended up spending a total of an entire year in the hospital, six months of which were in ICU. She had suffered a brain bleed, which is called a Traumatic Brain Injury. She had coded at one point, and had more surgeries during that year than I could even think about counting. So, the normal, happy, healthy, energetic four-year-old that walked in that hospital room in May of 2007 was wheeled out a year later in a wheelchair with more lines and tubes and medications than most people will ever see in their life. That was a really rough year, fighting for her life, but I sure learned a lot about what did not work well with our medical system. As you would imagine, at that point we were simply grateful she was alive.

After we got Taylor home from the hospital, I took on the task of weaning her off the 25 oral and IV medications that we had come home with. At that time, she had a pic line, a central line, a j-tube, a g-tube, and a trach. Her care was 24/7—administering meds and making sure she was cared for. It was by far the most challenging thing in my life but I have learned SO MUCH from that experience that I am forever grateful for. It took me a year and a half to wean her off all the meds and get all the tubes and lines out of her safely. (She still has her g-tube which serves as my way of getting all the proper nutrition into her body, but she does eat by mouth.... she is your typical picky teenager and loves spaghetti and mashed potatoes, and we all know that's not super healthy, even if organic.)

During this time, I was using many, many different types of nutritional supplements and juicing to detox her from the residual effects of the extreme amount of medications she had been on. I couldn't get all the fruits and veggies she needed that were packed full of phytonutrients, vitamins, minerals, and trace minerals through the juicer and into her tiny g-tube, so I used a powdered greens supplement. I will be honest with you, it tasted like mowed lawn and required I use 3 heaping tablespoons full each day to provide all of this for her (on top of the juicing). I even grew my own wheat grass to juice daily so you know I was serious about the BEST nutrition for her. As a family we would not consume this product due to the taste, but Taylor (with the tube to her stomach) had no idea what it tasted like, thank God, and it helped her immensely during those first couple years of detoxing.

In the summer of 2010, I ran into a longtime friend at the salon when I went in to get a haircut. She was excited to see me and said she knew she would be running into me soon! Have you ever had a "chance meeting"? You know, when you coincidently run into someone, but all along it was really a DIVINE appointment scheduled from above? Little did I know that one "hair cut" appointment would forever alter the course of my life in ways not even dreamt of. She knew I was juicing for Taylor and wanted to see if I would be open to taking a look at a powdered greens product she had that she thought would really benefit my daughter's health. Now, I don't know about you, but if someone tells me about something they think would benefit my child, I am going to at least look into it. What do I have to lose? Nothing! What do I have to gain? Possibly everything, but I won't know unless I try, and that is my philosophy!

Of course, before she would let me get some of this for Taylor, she wanted me to taste it. I've already shared with you what I thought of those powdered greens supplements, so I was not too keen on trying it, but she insisted that it was amazing. It actually was! The Greens product that I reference in Appendix A near the back of this cookbook is what she had me try that day, and I am forever grateful that I did.

It comes in berry or chocolate flavors. Berry tastes just like a fruit roll-up or grape Kool-Aid, and chocolate tastes just like cocoa powder, like you are having a chocolate milkshake. No vitamin aftertaste. No chalky gritty taste left in your mouth. I was sold! Not only for Taylor, but for the rest of the family, too. I knew the power of detoxification on a daily basis (from the pollutants in the air, the water, and our food), and the importance of keeping the pH of your body in balance. This product does just that and so much more!

After going home that day, my wheels started turning—I had learned so much in such a short period of time on this road to recovery with Taylor. I had already started teaching classes at local churches for moms requesting I share with them ways to get their kids healthy and to keep them healthy. I thought to myself…if I could share these affordable nutritional products with these moms and help alkalize and detox their kids safely and daily, then maybe, just maybe, I could prevent another child from going through what Taylor had to endure…if I only would have known then what I know now…

So, I decided to start sharing these amazing products with others looking to get and stay healthy and I joined It Works! Global. That is all I ever planned on doing and look at me now—over eight years later, writing a Vegan/Keto cookbook! Who would have thought it? Surely not I, but we just don't have all the plans laid out before us at every moment. We have to trust in God and in the process of life, and always work on learning and growing and being the best version of ourselves, all while making a positive impact in our lives and the lives of others.

As I said, I was first introduced in 2010 to the It Works!™ supplements and products you will see referenced in this cookbook. I have always been someone who uses different nutritional products. I love trying new things and I know that there is no way possible for me to get all the vitamins, minerals, and essential nutrients from the foods I eat, even eating the cleanest diet possible. Food is not like it was when I was growing up eating out of my mom's garden.

Keto Coffee makes mornings fun again

The soils are depleted, many nutrients are missing from our diet, and we just need a little extra help nowadays. Trust me when I say that I am an educator, I am a coach, I am a product tester, and an avid proponent when sharing something that I love—but I am not a salesperson. I love to help people feel better from the inside out. In this cookbook, there is nothing I mention in the recipes or in Appendix A which is included as an advertisement. Do I hope to persuade you to try what I have found so incredibly helpful to my daughter, to me, and to so many others? Yes. But to "sell" you? No. If you feel in your heart that you are led to try something out, fabulous; if not, fabulous. Please know that I have only included something if it is a product which I have found on my journey to be indispensable.

So...back to Miss Taylor. I dedicated myself to weaning her off all the medications by juicing, detoxing, and boosting her immune system, and I watched my little girl come back to life. Before her hospital admission, Taylor was a precocious over-achiever who loved to read and write and do basic math, even before kindergarten age. I used to be a teacher and I knew that getting back to those activities was crucial to her recovery and mental health. So Taylor and I started journaling together. I was so grateful that she still had that ability after everything that she had been through.

They say that people who have had a near-death experience have a unique perspective on life and I knew this to be true with Taylor after reading the countless journal entries she had written over the years. She has always been very in tune and wise beyond her years, so to be totally honest with you, I decided to become a vegan because I trusted that she knew something I didn't, but that I needed to learn. Looking back over the last several years, she has proven me right in a massive way that I know I'll never be able to fully comprehend. The ripple effect from the journal entry that Taylor made has radically changed my life in more ways that I can describe and I know it has impacted thousands, if not hundreds of thousands, of others through personal interactions and social media. This decision has been one of the best decisions of my life. I hope you will share with me the continuing, positive ripple effect it can have on your life as well.

Taylor, my ray of sunshine

Since coming home from the hospital, she has written journals upon journals of all sorts of information. But that day four years ago when she wrote that I should go vegan, that I had to give up my seafood and eat only veggies, I listened. I never dreamed or imagined that it would take me down this path and would lead to creating this cookbook, but here I am. Not only am I positive that this is what I am supposed to do, I am clear that ALL proceeds from here on out will go to the camp for special needs children that has become a true godsend in Taylor's life.

When we moved to Florida four years ago, we had no family here, no help or assistance whatsoever, but we knew we would find help from a college student or a neighbor. My husband and I, being entrepreneurs, sometimes have events in the evenings or on weekends that require us to seek help from someone who can keep an eye on Taylor.

Soon after settling into our Florida home, I met a woman who told me about a camp for special needs children. We were very skeptical in the beginning, of course. We had only brought people into our home that we had trained specifically on how to care for Taylor. We had never taken her anywhere and left her, so the thought of bringing her to a camp in the woods where she would stay in a cabin with other girls and counselors did not sound appealing, or even possible. But this woman assured me that her son had the time of his life every single time he got to go, and that it was the best place on the planet for kids with special needs. She said it gave her and her husband and their other children an opportunity to do things without the usual limitations when having a special needs child with them. I listened politely and thought, *okay, that's nice*…and then forgot about it.

Then I ran into her again, and again she prompted me to call the camp for Taylor. She acted like she was certain, without even knowing Taylor, that this camp was going to be the best thing for her. A "chance" meeting? I went online and I filled out the application this time, yet still felt skeptical. For sure, I wasn't going to take my child there and leave her on a weekend with strangers that I hadn't even properly trained. Some months went by and I ran into the woman yet again. This time she was insistent that Taylor needed to experience the fall session, which was about to start. My husband, Brent, started volunteering at the camp, helping out by cleaning sidewalks, gutters, and the like, so he could get a better feel for the people there and what this place was all about.

We decided one weekend to take Taylor out there during the day just on a Saturday, not to spend the night, but just to see what she thought of it during the day. When we went out to check on her, she was having a blast and was not really happy that we were there! We decided we would come back again later that evening before bedtime and see how she was doing.

Besides her writing, Taylor can communicate by saying "no," "Mom," "uh-huh," or by blinking her eyes to show whether she wants something or not. When we went back out to the camp that night before bedtime, she was adamant that she was not leaving. She was staying at that camp overnight. She wanted independence, she wanted freedom, and she wanted something to call her own. Taylor had spent the last eleven years of her life in a wheelchair. Up to this point, the only source of friendship had come from kids at school back in Indiana. The Dream Oaks Camp opened up a whole new world to Taylor that Saturday, a world that she wanted to explore. With the biggest, deepest breath, Brent and I walked away from that camp leaving our baby girl to spend the night with people she didn't even know.

I don't think we slept a wink that night. I don't know that she did either, but the next morning when we went to pick her up she was so happy. She wrote about her camp in her journal that day and how much she loved it and wanted to go back every single session.

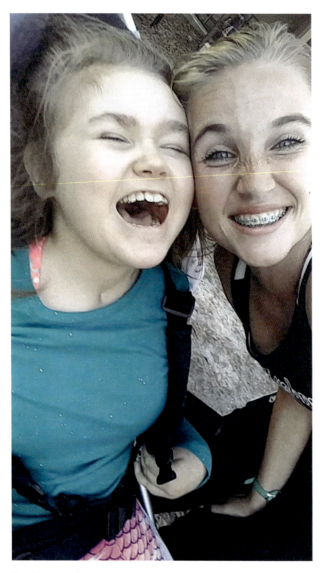

Taylor let us know she LOVED Dream Oaks Camp.

Dream Oaks Camp, where Taylor and friends can just have fun

Making "forever friends" at Camp

The Dream Oaks Camp is a place where kids like Taylor, kids with special needs, can express themselves with no judgment. Everybody loves everybody, no matter if they're mentally challenged, physically disabled, loud, shy, or quiet; everyone is loved the same. It's a place where kids can be themselves and have the same experiences that other kids do—playing games, doing crafts, singing music, dancing, playing dress-up, swimming, going on scavenger hunts, boating, canoeing, horseback riding—the list goes on and on. At this extraordinary place, these kids are spoiled rotten over the course of the weekend, or during the entire summer if they attended the weekly sessions at summer camp.

With that on my mind and in my heart, I have decided to donate all proceeds from this cookbook to the Dream Oaks Camp so that children who don't have the funds will be able to attend the camp on the weekend or during the summer. Every single dollar earned will help pay for a child to attend camp so they can experience the freedom, the joys, the fun that Dream Oaks Camp provides for kids with special needs—kids just like Taylor. By purchasing this cookbook, you have granted a child with special needs the opportunity to experience the life-changing world that Dream Oaks Camp has to offer. You've purchased at least a million smiles. Thank you.

INTRODUCTION

When I decided to cut out all gluten, dairy, and sugar four years ago, I never dreamed that within four months I would also completely cut all meat out of my life and go vegan. And never in my wildest dreams did I think I would be cooking healthy meals on a daily basis for my family. I am a busy mom of a 15-year-old special needs daughter on a specific diet and a 13-year-old son...who is both ravenous and super picky! I run a thriving health and wellness business where I help people from all over the country make healthy lifestyle changes every day. I had settled on eating as well as possible, when it was convenient, anyway.

But in the fall of 2015, I found myself at my wits end with my body. Over the previous four years of traveling, eating out in restaurants, and little time for exercise, I found myself approaching 40 and fat! I was coaching others how to get healthier, but I had lost touch with taking care of my own needs. As most women can relate, I assured myself that it wasn't that I was coming up on 40. And it surely wasn't that I had sensitivities to any foods...I wasn't going to be labeled as a person who had allergies or issues but, sure enough, when I hit rock bottom as the scale tipped over 215 pounds and climbing, I was desperate to try anything to get my body back. I was sick and tired of waking up in the morning with my eyes swollen shut and my fingers so fat I couldn't get my rings on.

Just when I couldn't take any more of my fatness, I saw a post on social media that led to a different future for me. It was like the heavens parted and there appeared a post by an acquaintance of herself with her family—and she looked fabulous. Happy, healthy, fit, and confident. She had hashtagged "Whole30" and I thought to myself that it must be nice to be a mom of four and look that good at 30. I clicked on the hashtag and that one click has radically changed my life. I saw a sliver of hope in that moment. I saw her "before" photo of what she looked like before she cut out gluten, dairy, and sugar, and then her "after" photo of what she looked like 30 days later. Yes, only 30 days! I was astounded and thought to myself, if she can do it then so can I... BOOM! My journey to a new, thinner, fitter, healthier, and happier me began that day. I went and did a little research, printed off some shopping lists, and went to the grocery store. I came home and threw out all the cheese and crackers, and all the chocolate and vodka! I was ready for the change. Staci 2.0 here I come!

I'm not going to lie; the first 30 days were not all roses and puppies! It took a solid three weeks to slay my "sugar dragon." I never really had a sweet tooth, but I loved my specialty chocolate bars and my weekend vodka and water. Well, three weeks in with none of the above and I could see a massive difference in my body. There are NSVs (non-scale victories) celebrated eating this way for 30 days, so I wasn't sure how many pounds I had lost, but I knew it was good. I was fully alive again with a renewed sense of hope that *all* of this excess weight was coming off! At the end of the 30 days I had dropped 20 pounds and two pant sizes. I was ecstatic! Throughout the month I had taken others on this journey with me through my social media posts and in person, and they watched the incredible, SIMPLE meals I was preparing and the transformation in my body that was taking place.

I am excited to say that the journey didn't stop there and, over the course of the next three months, I dropped another 15 pounds, joined my local gym, and started promoting this lifestyle change to literally thousands of people daily through my social media sites.

Fast forward three years and I am down 75 pounds forever, and in better shape than I have been in almost 25 years! I feel alive! I feel amazing! Know that if I can do this, so can you, and I'm excited to share these simple, easy but absolutely amazing recipes with you that I've found along the way.

Why Vegan?

As a child I always threw the meat off my plate and under the table to my toy poodle. How that little thing ate all of that meat each night I'll never know, but for me it was absolutely disgusting. I wanted no part of it. I was your typical carb kid. Give me all the mashed potatoes and pancakes any day but leave out the meat and veggies. As an adult I preferred seafood if I did eat meat and it really wasn't until I met my husband 22 years ago that I started eating steak. He was your typical country boy who lived off steak and potatoes, so when we would go out on the weekend, if I couldn't find really good seafood, I would get a bacon wrapped filet mignon. Once I had children a few years later even that changed and I could barely stomach beef at all.

I had no intention of ever being a vegan. We had a sitter once that was a vegan—she ate only oatmeal and canned vegetable soup. That's what I thought being a vegan meant and I loved food, really good food prepared in restaurants, way too much to go to that "lifestyle." You know those moments where you swear you will NEVER do something and then the universe conspires to make sure you do? Well I

INTRODUCTION

experienced that "moment" in early 2016 when I attended a Tony Robbins event.

I was taking a car full of girls that weekend and we were talking about the Sunday training and how it was focused on eating healthy and using healthy products. I swore in that moment out loud that I would never go vegan no matter what Tony Robbins said! Growing up my dad and grandfather hunted deer, squirrels, and rabbits, so I saw that process and was not bothered at all by it. My dad would go to the local farmers, purchase a cow, take it to the butchers and bring home a side of beef to put in the freezer for the winter. Even though I didn't want to eat any of the meats, there was nothing cruel or hurtful about that process. You know how you may know something but not really understand, or maybe not want to understand, the truth? I knew animals were being pumped with hormones, mass produced needlessly, but I wasn't prepared for what I saw that Sunday.

That day opened my eyes for sure. Tony showed us videos of what they do to chickens and cows, the living conditions, and how they mistreat the animals. I left that day vowing to never eat another chicken, pig, or cow. But to me, seafood was still okay. The fish are swimming around out there in the great big ocean, they get caught up, and poof, I eat them. I mean, I went fishing in the lake behind my home all the time as a child and caught tons of fish. There never seemed to be anything inhumane about that. Little did I know, these creatures are full of heavy metal neuro toxins like mercury and PCBs, not to mention the farm-raised versions are loaded with too many antibiotics and pesticides, and their living conditions are horrific.

Nonetheless, I still left thinking I would eat my wild caught salmon...until a few days later when I was writing with my daughter, as mentioned earlier. Even though she's in a wheel chair and has very limited speech, she can still write and has written journals and journals of such insightful information over the years. That day, we were writing about the clothes she wanted to buy and the new camp friends she had made when she mentioned the word vegan. I responded with a little laugh that I'd already given up gluten, dairy, sugar, and, most recently, all meat, except seafood—I thought that was good enough. I mean, what was left to eat but ICE at this point? But she insisted that I go vegan.

I told you the only vegan I knew ate oatmeal and soup. No thank you. She told me to get cookbooks and do it. As it turns out, cooking and eating vegan has been one of the easiest things I've ever done. Thanks to awesome apps, the internet, and other cookbooks like these, it made my life super easy. I'm all about incredible food, fast, so in this cookbook you will find just that. Of course, if you or someone in your family is not vegan, then you can sub any meat with no problem and no judgment.

Why Keto?

I lost a total of 55 pounds in the first six months with my new food choices, exercise routines and nutritional supplements. I was able to happily continue these practices and keep the weight off for almost two years. I never counted any carbs, calories, fats, or proteins during this time. I just listened to my body. If my stomach was upset after a meal or I ended up with gas by the end of the night, I didn't eat that food again or maybe tried it at a later date to see if it had the same effects.

In the fall of 2017, my company launched a first-to-market, all-in-one, on-the-go Keto Coffee™. Now mind you, at this point I had not been a coffee drinker; water and unsweetened green tea were how I stayed hydrated, with a once-a-month-splurge on a glass of really good red wine. I loved the way I was looking and feeling. I was at my goal weight and was feeling fab in my clothes. But I had decided that I wanted to get into the 150s…you know, that thing that hadn't happened since I'd had kids? Just five pounds would more than do the trick so I thought I'd give Keto Coffee™ a try. And WOW…after just one week of replacing my breakfast with the Keto Coffee™, I not only had unbelievable mental clarity, focus, and energy, but I had dropped that five pounds lickity-split.

I was super happy and thought I'd better do some research on keto—OMG—I had been eating a keto lifestyle for two years and didn't even know it was called that. No wonder I had kept the 55 pounds off and dropped literally 10 years from my face. So, vegan? Yes! Keto? Yes!

A ketogenic ("keto") diet is a low-carbohydrate, moderate-protein, high-fat diet. Calories come from roughly 75% fat, 20% protein, and 5% carbohydrate. By restricting your intake of carbohydrates and proteins, the keto diet kicks your body into a state of ketosis, forcing it to use fat as its main energy source. Your body is designed to store fats in preparation for times of an "energy shortage" so that fat can be metabolized and burned for fuel. Your body's first choice of calories to burn is carbohydrates, since these are quickly metabolized for ready energy. When the body does not have enough carbohydrates to use, it turns to the fat, and the ketosis system takes over. This is a natural process of your body that happens overnight when you're sleeping, between meals, when you're fasting, and even when you're sick. A ketogenic diet uses this natural physiology to help you burn stored fat. When your body is in ketosis, using fat as its source of energy instead of glucose from carbs, it will start to produce ketones, which is a breakdown of fat by the liver. The ketones are a by-product of fat metabolism and are a high-energy fuel source, particularly for your brain!

Keto means eating 20g of carbs or less a day (up to this point I had basically been eating around 50g a day, which wasn't too far off and why I was able to keep the weight off), a moderate lean protein (I have that covered with a vegan diet), and a lot of healthy fats (which I had been getting in the form of coconut oil, olives, olive oil, avocados, and avocado oil all this time. Not to mention, nuts and seeds were my besties!). I knew I could make this simple, science-based plan work perfectly…with a little work. For six months, things trucked along nicely. I experimented with all sorts of foods, found which ones made me feel unstoppable and which ones were just okay.

I want to mention that this is in no way shape or form the Adkins way of eating. I read his books 20 years ago and tried that for a short period of time. I could not stomach eating so much ground

INTRODUCTION

beef, sausage, fatty steak, processed meats, and cheeses. I felt like I was going to die and the 15-20 pounds that I wanted to lose at the time was not worth it to me. Too greasy…the opposite of clean eating! Also, I am not recommending any food choices as a professional dietitian, nutritional or medical person, although I've read an awful lot written by authorities. I am simply sharing with you what my research and personal testing has found to be true. My own results and those in my family are valid for us, and I hope you can achieve your desired outcomes, too.

I want to recommend to you Dr. Don Colbert's book, *The Keto Zone Diet*. It is not a "diet" book at all but an incredible easy-to-read reference guide developed from his 30+ years of experience on treating patients with everything from diabetes, high cholesterol, heart disease, cancer, and even weight loss. My philosophies and beliefs around a holistic healthy lifestyle align with his and I appreciate his viewpoints on eating a diet that is primarily plant-based, especially if you are suffering from health issues. Just remember that GOOD fats are healthy for you! You will see in these recipes GOOD and healthy fats which will fuel your brain and body.

At the beginning of 2018, It Works!™ launched our ketones product, "Ketones™." This is a lemon-flavored powder blend of amino acids and electrolytes. It tastes just like Country Time™ lemonade. I've written a section for you all about ketones, ketosis, and the keto diet (see "Why Keto?" on page 11.) After researching the benefits of exogenous ketones, I wanted to go all-in and implement them along with the coffee. I also introduced intermittent fasting to my world. HOLY COW! I dropped 17 pounds in six weeks and I could not believe how effortless it was. I would get on the scale each morning thinking I left some excess fat in the bed from the night before. I went on to lose another three pounds over the next couple of months, making little tweaks here and there, for a total of 75 whopping pounds GONE FOREVER!

I had no idea what intermittent fasting was until I decided to go strict keto/vegan. I have fasted many, many times in my life. I started when I got out of high school and was on my own. I had read about it in one of the health, fitness, or women's magazines that I subscribed to at the time. I think I have tried every fast on the market. With some of them I felt like I was under the ground, they were so bad! I do realize the importance of detoxing and cleansing the body at least 3-4 times a year, so when I learned that intermittent fasting would do that and oh-so-much more, I was intrigued, to say the least. I am all about feeling good, looking good, and anti-aging in the process. I am not going to go in depth about detoxification. I know you can find the information you are looking for just like I did, and find the fasting style that is right for you, but I did want to share a few of the key benefits so that you realize it can be a very beneficial part of your healthy LIFE!

Intermittent fasting is an eating style where you eat within a specific time period, and fast the rest of the time. I personally have followed the 16/8 rule for over a year now with tremendous results. I consume all my calories during an eight-hour period, then let my digestive system work and rest for sixteen hours. Though intermittent fasting is an effective way to lose weight, it's less of a *diet* and more of a *lifestyle choice*. This is so true. I have friends that do the 12/12 and others that only fast once a month. You have to find what works best for you. The benefits of intermittent fasting include: weight loss, protection against chronic disease, improved brain function, and increased longevity, to name a few.

You can experiment with different approaches to intermittent fasting. With Keto Coffee™ and intermittent fasting, I skip breakfast every morning and drink my Keto Coffee™ instead. The healthy fats from the grass-fed butter and MCT oil powder, coupled with the kick of caffeine and the added benefits of the collagen give you energy and keep hunger pangs at bay without switching on your digestion (food craving) for hours.

I cannot believe how I feel or look. I am the weight I was when I graduated college and I actually feel like I'm 24 years old again, too. I work out harder than the majority of people half my age and most days I feel like I could do it all over again, and some days I do. I know that I have almost perfected using my *food for fuel*. Doesn't that sound like what God had intended when our bodies were designed? It is the most natural way of eating, the cleanest way of eating, and, with the delicious recipes I am sharing with you in this cookbook, it's the most enjoyable and satisfying way of eating. So, allow these vegan/keto recipes to find their way into your life, whether you are just starting your journey, are looking to gain that upper edge, or you're somewhere in the middle. Wherever you are now, I can honestly say I know these types of foods can help you reach your goals and far exceed your wildest imagination of what you can accomplish if you will stay consistent and never give up on yourself. You are so worth it!

There are a few things more I would like to add before you dive into my favorite recipes. First off, if I happen to mention a brand name in a recipe it is because it is my favorite and I have tried some of the others and was not impressed with their flavors. We all have different tastes, so feel free to experiment with these recipes as I did, and find which brand names you like best. If you cannot find an item in your local stores, you'll almost certainly find it online.

INTRODUCTION

Next, when I prepare food I only use a paper plate and a steak knife to chop and cut the items in my recipes. I have found that I do not get along with sharp knives or cutting boards very well. With a serrated steak knife I know exactly what I am cutting and I can do it fast. I love using a paper plate to cut my veggies or tofu because it has a big round edge and holds everything in one place. With cutting boards, everything seems to slide off and onto the counter, sink, or floor, even if using the ones that have "lips." So be prepared when you start watching me cook on social media. Rather than try and copy a TV chef, me, or someone else, my advice is to find what works best for you.

And finally, I have been labeled the "Reckless Measurer" and I honestly feel that suits me perfectly! I go live on my social media several times a week where I typically prepare first-time recipes in front of thousands of people who watch me measure and pour each ingredient and proceed all the way to finish in no time flat. Many of them have joked with me that my tablespoons quickly turn into quarter cups, and my quarter cups turn into half cups—I am guilty of that for sure! When cooking live, on the spot, in front of tons of people who are actively commenting, asking questions, and me giving feedback, it is easy for a teaspoon to accidentally turn into a tablespoon without even realizing it. I always laugh it off and keep going! I have never had one recipe turn out gross or inedible…even if I am the Reckless Measurer. DO NOT stress out if you make a mistake while cooking. It's all good. There's room for error in these recipes. Enjoy the Grace!!

Healthy living has so many rewards!
(Yes, this is me, 3 years AFTER the BEFORE.)

Me with post-workout Keto Shake

Breakfast

Breakfast to me is the wonderful Keto Coffee™. Did you know that 64% of Americans drink coffee for their breakfast every morning? Why not make that coffee actually give you more health benefits than you imagined? Keto Coffee™ improves your mental clarity, focus, and energy. The essential fatty acids in it leave you feeling full for three to four hours. It consists of two different types of ground coffee, grass-fed butter, MCT oil powder, and collagen. It whips up to a creamy latte in seconds. But I do realize that things are always a little different on the weekends, and peoples' schedules do vary nowadays, so I've added a few breakfast options in here for those not-so-typical mornings.

I do want to mention that because I am a creature of habit, when I find something that really works, I rarely deviate from it; my mornings always start off with a 12-ounce glass of lemonade Ketones™ on my way to the gym, as you will see in my 14-day Meal Plan. When I return, I enjoy a cup of hot Keto Coffee™ and then I am full for three to four hours. I keep my mornings pretty simple no matter what day of the week it is.

My hubby, Brent, on the other hand loves to mix it up a lot so I'll be sharing his favorite breakfast shakes along with a couple others that I've successfully made for myself for lunches or snacks.

Clean Keto
Vegan Scrambled Eggs and Sausage

Sometimes you just want a little substance for breakfast...maybe after a night you enjoyed one glass of wine too many! This quick breakfast will not only fill you up but it will make you feel like you got this right off the menu at your favorite breakfast place.

Ingredients:

1 block extra-firm tofu
1½ T onion powder
¼ tsp turmeric
1 tsp smoked paprika
1 tsp mustard powder
¼ c nutritional yeast
1 T miso paste
½ c water
Salt and pepper to taste

Directions:

Crumble tofu into a large pan over medium-high heat.
Add the onion powder, turmeric, smoked paprika, and mustard powder to the tofu.
Sauté for one minute.

Add the nutritional yeast, water, miso, and a pinch of salt and pepper.
Sauté for two to three minutes.

While cooking, continue to scramble the tofu using a wooden spoon.

Taste-test and add additional salt, pepper or herbs to taste.

Serve with your favorite vegan sausage, prepared per directions on the package.

Breakfast

Blueberry Cinnamon Mug O'Muffin

This is one dish you will swear up and down is not keto—but I promise you it is! This becomes a meal for me sometimes—it's that good and filling. I absolutely love blueberries (but of course they could be substituted for strawberries, raspberries, or blackberries). I was that kid growing up...the one who would eat homemade blueberry pancakes every morning. My mom stayed home with us so a fresh, hot breakfast was served each day before she sent us off to school. Things are very different these days and some mornings we can barely get the kids out of bed, let alone have a hot, healthy breakfast. Well, stress no more! This little gem literally takes one minute to whip together and 1½ minutes to cook. I use wild Maine frozen blueberries, but you could use fresh berries of choice. (This may or may not be my late night go-to snack too!) Warm and sprinkle the golden monk fruit on top. It is just heavenly! Try to eat only one of these on your first attempt (ha!).

Ingredients:

1 T coconut flour
1 T almond flour
2 T golden monk fruit
1 tsp cinnamon
1 neat egg (prepared as directed)
1 T coconut oil
1 T unsweetened almond milk
3 T frozen blueberries

Directions:

In a small mixing bowl, combine the flours, sweetener, cinnamon and baking powder.
Add in your neat egg, almond milk, and mix until fully incorporated.
Fold in the blueberries and ensure there are a few remaining at the top.

For the microwave version, microwave for 1 minute and 30 seconds (or up to 2 minutes, depending on your microwave) and remove.
Enjoy immediately.

For the oven version, pour batter into an oven safe dish and bake at 350° for 12 minutes, or until a toothpick comes out clean.

Clean Keto

Vanilla Keto Shake

This is Brent's fast, easy go-to breakfast and it's oh so yummy, too. He has a major sweet tooth and this shake does the trick first thing in the morning for him. Plus, he found that having his Keto Shake means he is more focused and energized for the rest of the day. I get our daughter up and ready for school then head to the gym. He enjoys his shake while he feeds her breakfast and then they're off to school. Because of all the essential fatty acids (aka brain foods) that are in this Keto Coffee™ and shake, he is fueled up for his work day. Whether it's appointments, calls, or just chores around the house, this has him focused to get it all done before lunch, and feeling fab!

Ingredients:

1 scoop vegan vanilla protein shake (I use It Works!™)
1 package ready-to-go Keto Coffee™
1 c unsweetened almond milk
2 scoops chocolate It Works!™ Greens (a blend of 52 herbs and superfoods and 34 fruits and veggies)
Add ice, blend it, and enjoy!

Chocolate Lover's Delight

This is another simple, easy and super yummy shake for all you chocoholics out there, like me! This chocolate-almond butter protein shake has lots of healthy plant-based protein and good healthy fats to keep you full for hours. It definitely satisfies that sweet tooth without the sugar!

Ingredients:

1 scoop Rich Chocolate It Works! Shake™
2 T fresh almond butter
1 c unsweetened almond milk
¼ c Lilly's dark cocoa chips if you are as chocolate-crazy as I am!
Add ice, blend and enjoy

Breakfast

Creamy Strawberry Shake

One thing many people frown upon with keto is not being able to eat all the high-sugar fruits they are used to. And yes, most fruits are OUT with keto, but berries (in moderation of course) are not. This super yummy shake gives you all the frills of eating sweet fruit, but with the wonderful fats to keep you full for hours with no guilt.

Ingredients:

¼ c Go Veggie cream cheese
1 5-oz. can coconut cream
1 c frozen strawberries
2 T golden monk fruit sweetener
2 T unsweetened almond milk
Blend and enjoy!

Lemon Pound Cake Shake

Oh my sweet heavenliness—this tastes just like Starbucks™ lemon pound cake! This one is definitely my FAVORITE shake. I love lemon and vanilla and this combo together with a little bit of coconut creamer just hits the spot. It makes me super happy to integrate healthy nutritional products into my life in creative ways and this shake turned out to be just that…a super-charged, healthy slice of lemon amazingness.

Ingredients:

1 scoop Creamy Vanilla It Works! Shake™
1 scoop lemon Ketones™
1 scoop Perfect Keto coconut MCT oil powder or powdered creamer
½-1 c unsweetened almond milk
Add ice, blend and enjoy!

Clean Keto
Old Fashioned Keto "Oatmeal"

I loved oatmeal as a child, growing up. As I got older and started making my own breakfast, the maple and brown sugar oatmeal packs were my lifesaver. This recipe makes me think of those days...with a slightly healthier spin, of course.

Ingredients:

½ c water
2 T hemp hearts
2 T almond flour
2 T unsweetened shredded coconut
1 T flaxseed meal
1 T chia seeds
¼ tsp golden monk fruit
1 pinch sea salt
½ tsp pure vanilla extract
Cinnamon to sprinkle over the top

Directions:

Stovetop Method: Add all ingredients except the vanilla to a small saucepan over low heat. Cook until thickened, stirring constantly, about 3 to 5 minutes; stir in the vanilla.
Serve warm.

Microwave Method: Add all ingredients except the vanilla to a large cereal bowl that's microwave-safe.

Microwave on high until thickened, about 2 minutes; stir in the vanilla.
Serve warm.

Breakfast

Shake-and-Make Chocolate Mousse

Here I am again with the Rich Chocolate shake…but I truly love chocolate and it just makes my heart smile. I have also found that I love full-fat coconut milk. It's so creamy and rich and full of flavor. Enjoy this shake in the morning or any time you are on the go. Make it the night before… all you have to do is grab it out of the fridge and you are off to an incredible start to your day.

Ingredients:

1 c full-fat coconut milk
2 T cacao powder
2 T sugar-free maple syrup (Lakanto is my favorite)
1 tsp vanilla extract
Pinch of pink sea salt
1 T chia seeds

Directions:

Place the ingredients (in the order listed) into a mason jar or small blender cup with a lid.

Give it a quick stir and pop on the lid.

Shake somewhat vigorously at first and then give it a quick shake every couple of minutes for five or so minutes.

Place in the fridge for several hours or overnight.

Clean Keto
Crustless Mini Tofu Veggie Quiche

This is one that I enjoy making on the weekends because it takes a little more time and keeps well in the fridge all week long. Brent loves to snack on these little babies! They are easy to pop in the microwave for 30 seconds, and they satisfy you enough until that next meal.

Ingredients:

1 T olive oil
3-5 baby bella mushrooms, sliced
½ red bell pepper, diced
1 c Beyond Meat Beefy Beef Free Crumbles or vegan Italian sausage crumbled
1 c baby spinach
1 block extra firm tofu
3 T nutritional yeast
1 tsp dried herbs (basil, tarragon, rosemary, etc.)
¾ tsp Himalayan pink sea salt
½ tsp onion powder
½ tsp garlic powder
½ tsp paprika (regular or smoked)
¼ tsp ground turmeric
¼ tsp ground black pepper
¼ c water

Directions:

Heat olive oil in a skillet on medium heat.
Add beefy crumbles or vegan sausage, mushrooms, and bell pepper.
Sauté until soft and slightly browned, about 5 minutes.
Add spinach and cook another minute.
Remove from heat and allow to cool slightly.

Preheat oven to 425°.
In a food processor or NutriBullet®, blend tofu, nutritional yeast, herbs, salt, onion powder, garlic powder, paprika, turmeric, black pepper, and water.
This mixture will be very thick.
If it's too thick to process, add more water 1 T at a time until thin enough to blend.
Transfer tofu mixture to a large bowl and fold in sautéed mix.
Coat muffin tin with coconut or olive oil.

Breakfast

Scoop batter into muffin cups by ½ cup scoops.
Bake for 45-50 minutes, until a toothpick inserted in the middle comes out clean.
Let the quiche cool completely.
Use a fork to remove from muffin tin.
Transfer to an airtight container and store in refrigerator.

Optional, for a less wet quiche: Cool quiches 15-20 minutes in pan. Loosen quiches with a butter knife and invert onto a baking sheet (bottoms up). Broil on high 5-8 minutes, until golden. Cool before storing.

Main Meals

One of the things I love about these recipes is that they are all you need for your entire meal. And, not to mention, they are my all-time favorite dishes bringing all the flavors and all the frills, but in record time because this momma of two doesn't have time to stress over food in the kitchen all day. When I'm hungry I want to be eating in 15-20 minutes, 30 minutes max. And it better taste better than almost anything I've ever eaten, so that means I have to set my standards pretty darn high in the department of taste, texture, and time. These meals are sure to wow you every time. You know that when people come over to visit and they request that you make them time and time again, they are the real deal!

Clean Keto
Volcano Tempeh Tacos

This recipe is the "crown jewel" of all my recipes. It is featured on the cover of this cookbook for a reason. I've made these volcano tacos (as I like to call them) for many people—so many that I actually get frequent requests from people to come to their home and prepare this meal for them and their friends. You may be surprised to learn that I've actually done it a few times (this surprises me, too!), but it is not something I plan on doing on a regular basis. Cooking this way for myself and my hubby is a pretty new thing for me, so when I tell you I'm cooking for 10+ people, by request, you better know the recipe doesn't disappoint.

Ingredients:

For the tempeh mixture:

3-4 T olive or avocado oil (or more as needed)
1 block tempeh, crumbled
1 onion, diced
1-2 seeded jalapeños, diced
2-3 T smoked paprika
2-3 T cumin
2-3 T chili powder
(Use the above four ingredients to suit your taste for spiciness. Some like it hot!)
Himalayan pink sea salt to taste
Fresh cracked pepper

For the Avocado mixture:

2 ripe avocados
1 lime, juiced
6-8 cherry tomatoes, diced

For the Sriracha Mayo:

½ c Vegenaise™ Mayo
1-2 T powdered sriracha, depending on preference (I prefer Trade East brand)
Fresh spinach

Be Kind tortilla shells

Main Meals

Directions:

Heat the oil on medium-high heat.
Add in the onions and peppers until golden brown.
Add in the tempeh and spices.
Let simmer while preparing the rest.

Mash up the avocados.
Squeeze in the fresh lime juice.
Add in the diced tomatoes and stir.

In a separate bowl, mix the mayo and sriracha together.

To build your taco, start with the Be Kind tortilla shell (after you have browned it in the skillet with olive oil on medium heat.)

Add a layer of fresh spinach. Add a layer of tempeh. Top with fresh avocado. Drizzle sriracha mayo over the top like a volcano erupting and enjoy!

Volcano Tempeh Tacos...it's what's for dinner!

Clean Keto
Buddha Bowl

This little gem here is so easy and so flexible. I literally look in my fridge at the end of the week and pull out what's left as far as fresh veggies and protein. I throw it in the skillet with salt and pepper and sprinkle in the bowl. It just doesn't get much easier than that and the presentation is always incredible. Just think lots of color!

Ingredients:

Spinach (fresh, using amount you want to use as your base)
Tofu or tempeh cooked until golden brown in onions and jalapeños
Pink sea salt and pepper to taste
Broccoli
Carrots
Tomatoes
Olives
Or any mixture of veggies of choice
Top with fresh olive oil or homemade vegan ranch (see page 45).

Buddha's Delight   Buddha Bowl with Ranch

Main Meals

Chili Pepper Tempeh Stir-Fry

I throw all of this in the skillet and let it do its job. All of these ingredients should by now be staples in your pantry and fridge. As you can see, they can be used in many of the recipes but, interestingly, they vary enough that each tastes distinctly different.

Ingredients

For the Stir-Fry Sauce:

1 T toasted sesame oil
1 small hot chili pepper, minced
3 T sugar free ketchup
3 T tamari (reduced sodium)
2 T golden monk fruit
1 T fresh lime juice
1 tsp grated fresh ginger root
¾ c vegetable broth

For the Stir-Fry:

1½ T avocado oil or coconut oil
8 oz. tempeh, crumbled
1 small onion, diced
4 c fresh seasonal veggies or veggie mixture, such as broccoli florets or cut carrots
3 medium red, orange and/or yellow bell peppers, seeded, julienned
3 large garlic cloves, minced
3 scallions, chopped
¼ c slivered almonds
Fresh cilantro leaves, for garnish

Directions:

For the Stir-Fry Sauce:

Fully heat the sesame oil in a large saucepan over medium heat.
Add the hot pepper and sauté until fragrant, about 1 minute.
Add the ketchup, tamari, monk fruit, lime, ginger, and broth and reduce sauce mixture to slightly thicken, about 10 minutes.
Set aside. (Note: This stir-fry sauce can be made in advance and chilled.)

For the Stir-Fry:

Fully heat the avocado oil in a skillet over high heat.
Add the tempeh and onion and stir-fry until the tempeh is golden brown, about 3-5 minutes.
Add the seasonal veggies (such as broccoli), bell peppers, and garlic and stir-fry until the vegetables are heated through, about 5 minutes. Enjoy!

Clean Keto
Buffalo Tempeh Wings

I love spicy foods! If you don't you can still make this one amazing, just don't use as much hot sauce as I do. With football season being a big time for neighborhood parties, this one fools those boys on game days every time! I make these a meal often just by adding fresh veggie sticks and my homemade ranch dressing for dipping.

Ingredients:

½ c hot sauce
3 T vegan butter
1 package tempeh
Veggies of choice
Homemade ranch dressing [page 45] for dipping

Directions:

For the Buffalo Sauce:

Combine the hot sauce and butter in a small saucepan over medium heat.
Whisk until the butter is melted, sprinkle with salt, and remove from heat.

Prepare the Tempeh:

Add 1-2 T olive oil to skillet.
Slice the tempeh into thin strips, about 1 inch thick.
Toss the sliced tempeh in Buffalo sauce and transfer to the skillet.
Sprinkle with salt and pepper and marinate for 10 minutes.
Garnish with veggie sticks and homemade ranch dressing (see page 45).

Main Meals

Lemon Caper Cauliflower Steaks

You know men and their "steaks." This recipe is one that makes my hubby think he's eating a scrumptious steak from the steakhouse. Well, not really, but it's the closest thing he's getting in this house! I absolutely love lemon and caper together and this lemon butter sauce is so rich and creamy it just hits the spot.

Ingredients:

1 head cauliflower
8 oz. asparagus
½ c pumpkin seeds
1 shallot
3 T vegan butter
1 T capers
1 lemon
½ c raw spinach

Directions:

Prepare the Cauliflower:

Set your oven to broil on high.
Trim the leaves and about 1 inch of stem off the cauliflower, leaving the whole head intact.
Slice the cauliflower, from the top down, into 1-inch thick steaks.
On a baking sheet, gently coat both steaks in 1 T olive oil and season with salt and pepper.
Place on the middle rack and broil until well-browned, about 18 to 24 minutes.

Clean Keto

Roast the Asparagus:

Trim about 1 inch from the bottom of the asparagus.

Once the cauliflower has been roasting for 15 minutes, add the asparagus to one side of the baking sheet and toss with 1 teaspoon olive oil.

Sprinkle with salt and pepper and roast until bright green and just tender, about 6 to 8 minutes. At this point, the cauliflower should be well-browned.

Prepare the Lemon Butter:

Set your skillet to medium heat with 1 T olive oil.

Peel and mince the shallot, then add to skillet and cook until slightly softened, about 2 to 3 minutes.

Add the butter and capers, and stir until the butter has melted, about 1 minute.

Zest the lemon, and then halve it.

Add the juice from half the lemon and a pinch of salt, and stir to combine.

Bring to a simmer and then remove from the heat.

Serve:

Cut the remaining lemon half into wedges.

To serve, spread the spinach onto plates and top with the cauliflower steaks and roasted asparagus.

Drizzle with lemon caper butter and sprinkle with toasted pumpkin seeds and lemon zest.

Serve with lemon wedges.

Main Meals

Veggie Pad Thai

Not every meal requires you to add a protein item to it, and this veggie dish shows you just that. It's super filling and super yummy at the same time. And, of course, I love how quickly I can whip this one together, even for a quick lunch.

Ingredients:

6 oz. baby bok choy
4 oz. green beans
1 red bell pepper
3 scallions
Fresh cilantro
1 package Pasta Zero
¼ c slivered almonds
1 lime
2 T fresh almond butter
3 T tamari
1 T chili paste

Directions:

Trim the bok choy and roughly chop.
Cut the green beans in half.
Deseed and thinly slice the red bell pepper.
Chop the scallions into 2 inch pieces.
Chop the cilantro leaves and tender stems.
Cook the Pasta Zero according to the package.
Toast the almond slivers for 4-6 minutes on medium heat.

Sauté the Vegetables:

Heat a large skillet to medium-high heat with 1 T olive oil.
Once hot, add the bok choy, green beans, red bell pepper, and scallions.

Clean Keto

Sprinkle with salt and cook, stirring frequently, until the bell pepper is tender and the bok choy and green beans are bright green, about 3 to 4 minutes.

Add the Sauce:

In a medium bowl, whisk together the juice from the lime, almond butter, tamari, ⅓ c hot tap water, and as much of the chili paste as you'd like.
Add the sauce to the skillet with the vegetables, and then add the cooked Pasta Zero noodles. Reduce heat to medium and cook, tossing frequently, until the noodles are heated through, about 2 to 4 minutes.

Serve:

Divide the vegetable pad thai between plates.

Sprinkle with toasted almonds and chopped cilantro.

Jackfruit Nachos Supreme

Holy cow, hold on to your seats! You will completely flip your lid when you eat this meal. I mean flip! It has the texture of pulled pork and I guarantee you no one will know the difference. My first attempt at it my hubby had been boating all day with his friends and they all decided to come back to our house afterwards. I had literally just finished making these for myself when in they walk. They made themselves huge platters of loaded nachos, of course with (cashew) nacho cheese. They each had a heaping plate fully loaded all the way up and came back for seconds, never knowing it was all vegan. Fooled them! This is one of my husband's favorites, too. He loves Mexican dishes!

Ingredients:

For the Nacho Cheese:

¾ c raw cashews, boiled for 10 minutes, water reserved
¼ c nutritional yeast
2 T chopped canned green chilies
2 T lime juice
2 tsp white miso
1 tsp garlic powder
1 tsp cumin
¼ tsp turmeric, optional
Salt to taste

Main Meals

For the Nachos:

2 20-oz. cans jackfruit packed in brine (not syrup)
1 tsp extra-virgin olive oil
3 garlic cloves, minced
½ large onion, chopped
1 red bell pepper, chopped
2 T chopped canned green chilies
¼ c liquid aminos
¼ c tomato paste
2 tsp liquid smoke
1 tsp cumin
1 tsp smoked paprika
½ tsp ancho chili powder
Smoked salt or regular salt to taste
Black pepper to taste

Keto tortilla chips:

2 Be Kind tortillas lightly browned in the skillet with olive oil and cut into wedges

Tofu Sour Cream:

1 12-oz. package extra-firm silken tofu
¼ c fresh lemon juice
2 tsp apple cider vinegar
2 tsp white miso
2 tsp vegan mayonnaise

Directions:

Combine the nacho cheese ingredients, including ½ cup of the reserved soaking water, in a food processor or blender and process until smooth.
Cover until ready to serve.
Place the jackfruit in a colander and rinse thoroughly.
Use two forks or your fingers to tear it into shreds.
Set aside.

Clean Keto

Heat the oil in a large skillet over medium heat.
Add the garlic and sauté for 1 minute.
Add the onion and sauté until translucent.
Add the bell pepper and green chilies and sauté until the bell pepper is tender, about 5 minutes.
Meanwhile, mix the liquid aminos, tomato paste, liquid smoke, cumin, paprika, and chili powder in a cup.
Add the shredded jackfruit to the pan and sauté for a couple more minutes before adding the tomato paste mixture.
Stir to combine and simmer for about 10 minutes, until heated through and the sauce has thickened.
Add smoked salt and pepper; remove from the heat.
Spread the tortilla wedges on a large plate or platter.
Top with the jackfruit.
Drizzle the nacho cheese over the top.
Top with tofu sour cream and/or guacamole, if using.
Sprinkle with the green onions.
Serve immediately.

Coconut Curry Palmini-Linguine

I love coconut curry, you know that, but this one is not a soup. Yay! The base ingredients are obviously different. This recipe has more of an Asian flavor that I love, and with added noodles it makes it much thicker.

Ingredients:

1 can palmini noodles (hearts of palm noodles)
1-2 T curry paste (red or green, green is spicier)
2 T golden monk fruit
2 T tamari
1 tsp paprika
1 lime
1 12 oz. can coconut cream
½ c fresh basil
1 onion
Olive oil
Cilantro, for garnish

Main Meals

Directions:

In a large skillet add the olive oil and onion and cook until translucent.
Add the curry paste, coconut cream, tamari, monk fruit, paprika, basil (shredded), and lime juice.
Heat for 2-4 minutes, add the palmini noodles and simmer for 5-7 minutes until heated all the way through.
Top with cilantro and fresh squeezed lime.

Stuffed Portabella Mushrooms

Another yummy recipe that uses tempeh. You may wonder why I use this so much. Tempeh is one of those easy and fast foods to make and it's so versatile it goes well in anything. Most people would never even realize that it's not ground beef on their plate if you didn't tell them. It's such a healthy alternative to meat, and it's really good for your gut, too.

Ingredients:

Portabella Mushrooms
Olive oil
¼ tsp minced garlic
1 onion
2 T nutritional yeast
¼ tsp pink sea salt
1 block tempeh

Directions:

Clean out the mushrooms and set to the side to dry out.
In a large skillet add 3-4 T olive oil, garlic, and onion. Cook until fragrant.
Add the crumbled tempeh and sea salt, cook until the tempeh is browned up.
Add the nutritional yeast, mix together and spoon into the mushroom caps.
Bake at 425° for 15-20 minutes, or until mushrooms are done.
I like to make a side of veggies with this one, or a simple salad.

Clean Keto
Avocado Stuffed Tacos

OMG! This is avocado heaven for sure. Who would ever have thought to scoop out almost all of the fresh insides of an avocado and add in taco "meat"? Top these babies with my creamy avocado dressing and you will become a happy camper for sure!

Ingredients:

4 avocados
1 pkg. tempeh
2 T smoked paprika
2 T cumin
2 T chili powder
1 onion, minced
1 jalapeño
1 T cilantro
Juice of 1 lime
Cherry tomatoes
Salt and pepper to taste

Avocado Cream Sauce:

2 avocados, sliced and seeded
¾ c unsweetened almond milk or avocado oil
1 T fresh lime juice
2 cloves garlic, minced

Directions:

Cook crumbled tempeh until browned with all the ingredients listed.
Let simmer for 5-7 minutes while making the avocado cream dressing.
For the dressing, place all the ingredients in a blender or NutriBullet® and blend until creamy. Cut the avocados in half, take out the seed and discard.
Scoop out ¼ of the avocado and mash it in a bowl, then add the tempeh mixture to each avocado half. Garnish with the cherry tomatoes, mashed avocado, avocado dressing, and cilantro.

Main Meals

Tempeh Meatballs with Homemade Marinara over Pasta Zero

Ingredients:

1 onion
1 clove minced garlic
1 T nutritional yeast
¼ c almond slivers
1 T tamari
1-2 T water
1 tsp fresh basil
Olive oil
Sea salt and pepper to taste

Directions:

Heat oven to 425°.
Combine all ingredients in a bowl and mix with a spoon or by hand.
Roll into balls, should make 8.
Cook for 20 minutes.
Cook the Pasta Zero per package directions.
(See page 44 for homemade marinara recipe.)
Add the marinara to the noodles.
Top off noodles with cooked meatballs.

Clean Keto
Hempseed and Pistachio Crusted Cauliflower Steaks

Have you ever had breaded cauliflower as an appetizer in a restaurant? This recipe will make you think you are enjoying that deep-fried veggie but instead you are having a much healthier and oh-so-much tastier version of this! I actually make these my entire meal and, because of the wonderful amount of protein and fat in the seeds and pistachios, you can definitely do the same and feel satisfied.

Ingredients:

2 tsp olive oil
½ tsp coconut oil
½ c hemp seeds
¼ c pistachios
Zest from 1 lemon
1 medium-large head of cauliflower
Sea salt and pepper, to taste

Directions:

Chop cauliflower head into steaks by first removing outer leaves and slicing the cauliflower head in half. Depending on the size and shape of the cauliflower, you should be able to get 3-4 steaks out of it. Make sure the slices are thick enough so that most of the florets on the steak stay intact.
You can leave some of the stalk.
In a food processor, grind pistachios into small chunks, about the same size as the hemp seeds, and mix in a bowl with hemp seeds and 2 teaspoons olive oil.
The mixture should be slightly soft, but not too oily.
Set aside.

Season cauliflower with salt and pepper to taste.
Heat your skillet/grill pan over medium-high heat with a bit of coconut oil.
Once the pan is hot, add your cauliflower steaks, as many as will fit comfortably.
Sear them for approximately 3-4 minutes on each side.
Add each seared piece to a parchment-lined baking sheet as they are ready.
Heat oven to 425°.
Once you're all done searing each piece, grab your hemp-pistachio crust and start pressing it on top of one side of the cauliflower steak.
The oil you added to the mixture will help this stick to the cauliflower and help it to not burn while it's in the oven.
Now add the lemon zest over top and pop the baking sheet into the oven.
Roast for 15 minutes at 425° and then reduce heat to 300° for approximately 5-7 minutes.
The edges of the cauliflower should be browned slightly and you should be able to easily stick the middle with a fork.
If you want it softer, you can keep it in a little longer, but keep an eye on it so the crust doesn't burn.

Spaghetti Squash with Veggie Marinara

This is one recipe where you will have to think ahead a bit because the spaghetti squash needs to be cooked first for an hour. The trick is to throw it in the oven when you get home, and then about 15 minutes before it's done, whip the rest of this up! It's so simple to just throw some veggies in the skillet and sauté them with the marinara all in one. I'm all about making things fast and simple, for sure.

Ingredients:

1 medium spaghetti squash
1 T olive oil
3 cloves of garlic, minced
1 yellow onion, chopped
½ medium yellow bell pepper, chopped
1 package tempeh, crumbled
2 c canned diced tomatoes
2 T tomato paste
1 T red wine vinegar
1 tsp dried oregano
1 tsp ground pepper
Salt to taste

Clean Keto

Directions:

Bake the spaghetti squash at 425° for one hour before. At 45 minutes start cooking your tempeh mixture.
Heat large skillet with olive oil, onion, and garlic until translucent.
Add in yellow peppers and cook 3 minutes.
Add in tempeh and cook until golden brown.
Add in the remaining ingredients and simmer until spaghetti squash is finished.
Cut open and spoon squash onto plate.
Spoon desired tempeh mixture on top and enjoy!

Buffalo Tempeh Nuggets

I serve this recipe over cooked veggies and Pasta Zero, but you could also just put it on a bed of spinach and garnish with fresh veggies. The sauce acts as a dressing, so nothing extra is needed. At this point you might have guessed that I'm in love with savory and spicy dishes. Along this journey to better health I have found that I can taste every ingredient included in these meals, and the little kick I get from the spicy additions makes me feel like I can actually feel my metabolism revving up! Who doesn't want that, right?

Ingredients:

1 package of tempeh, cut into bite-sized chunks
1 tsp powdered sriracha (or more if you like it extra spicy-Trade East is my favorite brand.)
1 tsp mustard
1 garlic clove
1 tsp lemon juice
1 tsp tamari
1 tsp paprika
½ tsp cayenne pepper or chili pepper
½ tsp Italian seasoning
1 T water
Salt and pepper

Directions:

Heat large skillet on medium-high heat with olive oil and garlic until fragrant.
Add in the tempeh and heat until golden brown.
In a small mixing bowl add the other ingredients and whisk until smooth.
Add to tempeh and simmer 7-10 minutes.
Enjoy over a bed of spinach or with a side of roasted or stir-fried veggies.

Ginger Sesame Lettuce Wraps

When I am deciding on what I want for lunch or dinner, I take a minute to ask myself what I'm in the "mood" for and then start searching my fridge or pantry. With this recipe my taste for Asian cuisine is satisfied for sure. I also love how versatile the veggies can be in this one so I feel free to mix it up a little.

Ingredients:

For the Sesame Ginger Sauce:

¼ c water
¼ c tamari (I like to use low sodium)
3 T Lakanto sugar free maple syrup
1 tsp toasted sesame oil
1 T fresh grated ginger
1 clove garlic, minced

For the Lettuce Wraps:

Large leaf lettuce
1 T olive oil
1 c shredded carrot
1 c diced red pepper
1 c diced snow peas
1 package tempeh, crumbled

Directions:

Place all of the sesame ginger sauce ingredients into a small bowl and whisk until combined. Heat a large skillet over medium heat and add the olive oil.
When the oil is hot, add the carrot, red pepper and peas.
Cook for 3 minutes, stirring occasionally, and then add the crumbled tempeh.
Continue to cook for another 3 minutes and then pour in the sauce.
Stir until everything is combined and cook until sauce is thickened, 7-10 minutes.
Let the mixture cool for a few minutes (to avoid wilting the lettuce), and then spoon the mixture into lettuce cups.
Garnish with almond slivers and green onions.

Main Meals

Veggie Pizza (Yes, Pizza!)

This pizza uses the avocado chips (see page 53) as the crust, which make it taste heavenly! Of course, you can top this pizza with whatever you want. I love to add as many veggies to my meals as possible. It is fine to sprinkle on vegan "cheese" if you like. I don't personally feel the need to, but I do love adding nutritional yeast as a cheesy topper.

Ingredients:

Vegan Pizza Sauce:
1 27-oz. can whole tomatoes
15 fresh basil leaves, shredded
2 cloves garlic, peeled
1 T onion powder
¼ tsp dried oregano
¼ tsp red pepper flakes
½ tsp pink sea salt

Directions:

Add all sauce ingredients into NutriBullet® and mix.
Add pizza sauce to the cooked crust and top with veggies of choice, such as olives, peppers, spinach, or basil. Bake at 425° for another 5-7 minutes, or until the cheese is melted and the veggies are cooked.

Clean Keto
"Sausage" Stuffed Peppers

For this recipe I actually buy the ground vegan sausage and the Follow Your Heart vegan cheese. I typically like to make things from scratch (that sounds so weird to say!) but in this case I just ground up the "sausage" and went with it. This is a quick put together but does require you to bake it for a lot longer than I normally like to wait to eat. But, trust me, it's worth the wait! You can even make these on a Sunday and heat them for dinner Monday night.

Ingredients:

1 small onion, chopped
2 cloves garlic, minced
2 packages vegan Italian or other variety vegan sausage, ground
Black pepper, to taste
Splash of Bragg Liquid Aminos
14 oz. firm tofu, pressed, drained, and crumbled
2 T nutritional yeast
½ tsp dried thyme
¼ tsp turmeric
¼ tsp salt
¼ tsp smoked paprika
¼ c parsley, chopped
4 large bell peppers, seeded and centers removed
6-8 slices vegan cheddar cheese

Directions:

Preheat the oven to 425° and line a 9 x 13-inch baking pan with foil.
Add the crumbled tofu, nutritional yeast, thyme, turmeric, salt, smoked paprika, and pepper to a large bowl and stir to combine and set aside.
In a large skillet over medium-high heat, add a splash of water or vegetable broth and sauté the onion for 3-5 minutes..
Stir in the garlic, vegan sausage, and a pinch of sea salt and black pepper.

Cook until sausage is browned
Remove the mixture from the pan and set aside while you prepare the tofu.
Put the tofu mixture into that same pan and add a splash of vegetable broth, water, or tamari, depending on your taste. Cook, stirring often, until heated through.
Place the bell peppers into the prepared pan and divide the filling between them.
Cover tightly with foil and bake for 40-45 minutes, or until the peppers are tender.
If you like, place one slice of vegan cheese on top of each pepper.
Set the oven to broil and, watching carefully, melt and lightly brown the cheese.

Clean Keto
Zucchini Meatballs with Marinara over Pasta Zero

Sometimes you just want an amazing plate of "spaghetti." My hubby loves spaghetti. He's the guy who eats the noodles raw while he's cooking. I, on the other hand, always loved the marinara part of it. This recipe is going to give you all of that without the unwanted carbs.

Ingredients:

1 c shredded zucchini
1 c (120g) chopped walnuts
¼ tsp salt
1 T psyllium husks
1 T Italian seasoning
1 T dried oregano
¼ tsp granulated garlic
¼ tsp red pepper flakes

Directions:

Preheat your oven to 425° and line a baking sheet with parchment paper.
In a medium mixing bowl, stir together grated zucchini, chopped walnuts, and salt. Let this mixture sit for about five minutes to allow for some of the moisture to be pulled out of the zucchini.
Make Pasta Zero noodles as directed on package.
Add in the psyllium and seasoning, and stir until thoroughly combined. Let this sit for another five minutes, so the psyllium can start to bind.
Form golf ball-sized balls with your hands and place them on the baking sheet.
Bake for 30-35 minutes, until the zucchini balls are slightly brown on the outside and firm to the touch.
Serve over Pasta Zero noodles or shirataki noodles with homemade marinara sauce (see page 44). Enjoy!

Tofu Coconut Curry Soup

You will not find many soup recipes in this book because I am just not a soup girl, but, I have a soft spot when it comes to coconut curry. I love full fat coconut milk. It's so rich and creamy and I absolutely love spicy things, so the curry gives this recipe a nice little, sweet kick that just puts a smile on my face.

Ingredients:

1 16-oz. package tofu
Olive oil
½ onion, minced
2 T curry powder
1 T curry paste (green or red)
1 stalk lemon grass
1 can full-fat coconut milk
1 T Lakanto monk fruit
Juice of 1 lemon
Shredded carrots
1 bunch broccoli
1-2 zucchini
Salt and pepper to taste

Directions:

Cube tofu and brown evenly in a skillet with olive oil for ten minutes. While tofu is cooking, heat olive oil in separate large sauce pan with onion until light brown. Crush lemongrass and add into sauce pan, then add coconut milk and simmer for 3-5 minutes. Cook veggies in olive oil for 3-5 minutes.
Add curry, monk fruit, salt, pepper, and lemon juice to the sauce pan.
Simmer for 3-5 minutes and then add in tofu.
Simmer until thickened to consistency desired. Enjoy!

Clean Keto
Homemade Marinara Sauce

Ingredients:

1 28-oz. can whole San Marzano tomatoes (I use my mom's fresh canned tomatoes)
¼ c extra-virgin olive oil
4 garlic cloves, peeled and slivered
1 small dried whole chili or pinch crushed red pepper flakes
1 tsp pink sea salt
1 large fresh basil sprig, or ¼ tsp dried oregano, more to taste

Directions:

Mix all ingredients in a sauce pan and simmer 7-10 minutes until fragrant.

Ginger Sesame Marinade

Ingredients:

¼ c tamari
¼ c rice vinegar
2 T lime juice
2 T golden monk fruit
1 T minced fresh ginger
2 tsp toasted sesame oil
2 tsp sriracha or similar hot sauce
2 cloves garlic, thickly sliced

Directions:

Add all ingredients to a skillet and simmer for five minutes.
Pour over tofu and veggies.

Main Meals

Vegan Ranch Dressing

This is so quick and easy it doesn't even seem possible. But I have included a longer recipe here just in case you think you need to make your ranch more complicated. We are so used to looking at long paragraphs for the ingredients that this may seem too easy. But, trust me, you will love this even more for its simplicity!

See pages 22 and 24 for a couple of the many ways in which this very versatile dressing can be used.

Ingredients:

Basic Ranch Dressing:

½ c vegan mayo (Vegenaise™ tastes best to me)
1 tsp garlic powder
1 T fresh dill

Dressed Up Ranch Dressing:

½ c hemp hearts
½ c water
¼ c fresh dill
2 T nutritional yeast
2 T apple cider vinegar
Sea salt to taste

Directions:

Blend in NutriBullet® and enjoy!

Basil Pesto Sauce

Ingredients:

2 T tahini
2 T hemp seeds
½ lemon, juiced
1 small garlic clove
1 large handful fresh basil
¼-½ c water

Directions:

Mix all ingredients in a NutriBullet® and enjoy!

45

Snacks, Appetizers, and Side Dishes

I find these recipes are great ways to introduce non-vegan/keto people to this healthy lifestyle because they have such incredible flavors and they are so quick and easy to prepare! If you have a party to attend, or are having friends over, try one or two of these out on them. I guarantee you they will be asking for your recipe! I used to wait tables in college and I would always order off of the appetizer menu as my meal, and I find myself with some of these recipes making them into my meals too! Some things never change!

Clean Keto
Avocado Hummus

I love hummus. It's so yummy to dip veggies in but the chick peas always make it too high in carbs to be keto...but, this baby here is the bomb! You will keep this in your fridge all the time...if it doesn't all get eaten right away. Enjoy, guilt-free!

Ingredients:

2 avocados
½ fresh lemon juice
2 cloves garlic
½ T tahini
¼ tsp cumin

½ tsp sea salt
Pinch of cayenne (or not, if you don't want the kick)
Ground pepper
2 T olive oil

Directions:

Blend all ingredients in the NutriBullet® and enjoy with fresh veggies!

Broccoli Pizza Sticks

If you love pizza like I do, then you will love these pizza sticks with my fresh homemade marinara. Oh yes! They are made with broccoli, but I promise you they won't taste like it. And, if you share these with friends, they will have no idea either. These are also a sweet way to get your kids to eat veggies. Shhh…

Ingredients:

1 head of broccoli
1 "neat egg" (prepared according to package)
1½ c shredded mozzarella
¼ c freshly grated parmesan
2 cloves garlic, minced
½ tsp dried oregano
Pink sea salt to taste
Freshly ground black pepper
Pinch crushed red pepper flakes
2 tsp freshly chopped parsley
Warmed marinara, for serving (see page 44)

Directions:

Heat oven to 425°.
Line a baking sheet with parchment paper.
Clean and cut broccoli and "rice" it in your food processor or NutriBullet®.
Microwave riced broccoli for 1 minute to steam.
Carefully ring out extra moisture from the broccoli using paper towel or cheese cloth.
Transfer broccoli to a large bowl and add the neat egg, 1 cup mozzarella, parmesan, and garlic. Season with oregano, salt, and pepper.
Transfer dough to baking sheet and shape into a thin, round crust.
Bake until golden and dried out, 20 minutes.
Top with remaining ½ cup mozzarella and bake until cheese is melted and crust is crispy, 10 minutes more.
Garnish with parsley and pepper flakes, if using.
Serve warm with marinara.

Clean Keto
Vegan/Keto Granola

Because everyone needs some granola in their life! I first tried this recipe when I attended a good friend's sip-n-see for her newborn son. I always eat before I go anywhere because I never know what they will offer and don't expect anyone to make something special to suit my needs. Well, I was overly ecstatic to learn that this recipe was not only keto but also vegan. WIN WIN! And, it's oh-so-heavenly with a cup of Keto Coffee™! Thank you to my dear friend, Kaye Dixon, for sharing this gem with me...and all of you!

Ingredients:

2 c chopped walnuts
1 c chopped pecan pieces
1 c almond slices
½ c shredded coconut
1 T chia seeds
1 T ground flaxseed
1 tsp golden monk fruit
½ tsp nutmeg
1 tsp cinnamon
1 tsp vanilla extract
1 T MCT oil (or coconut oil)
¾ c sugar-free maple syrup
(Lakanto is what I use)

Directions:

Preheat oven to 325°.
Mix all ingredients together in a large bowl, slowly adding the maple syrup at the very end.
Cover a large baking sheet with parchment paper.
Spread the granola flat in the parchment paper.
Bake for 15 minutes, remove and gently mix the granola around.
This keeps it from burning.
Bake for another 15 minutes until done.
Sprinkle with extra monk fruit if you like it sweeter like I do!

Snacks, Appetizers, and Side Dishes

Tomato Basil "Fat Bombs"

If you know anything about a ketogenic diet, you know (and love) "fat bombs," sometimes called "keto bombs." These are snacks or items made with more healthy fat ingredients than protein or carbohydrates, and are a keto favorite because of their tastiness and ability to keep you feeling full.

This is one of those recipes I looked at and thought, Yuck, I can't imagine a 'fat bomb' that's not sweet and rich like my chocolatey ones I eat every day. But I was pleasantly surprised. And, actually, I didn't make mine into fat bombs at all! I wanted to leave the name for the "shock value" effect it had on me. But, it is quite creamy and yummy. This recipe is the perfect "dip" to take to a party or to keep in the fridge to snack on with the Nooch Crackers on page 54. Be sure to take this one to your parties and surprise all your non-vegan friends.

Ingredients:

1 package Go Veggie cream cheese, softened
¼ c nutritional yeast
¼ c marinara sauce (see page 44)
2 T chopped fresh basil leaves
Sliced cherry tomatoes, for garnish
Fresh basil leaves, for garnish

Directions:

Place cream cheese, nutritional yeast, marinara sauce and basil in a bowl and combine until smooth.
Cover the bowl with plastic wrap or air tight container and place in the fridge to chill overnight.

Clean Keto
Spinach and Artichoke Dip

I'm all about cooking fast on my cook top and this recipe is just that. In 10 minutes you can have a hot vegan dip that everyone will go crazy over, even your pickiest eaters. I love to throw everything together in my largest skillet and let it do the work. Simple, fast, and oh-so-satisfying. I like to use the Nooch Crackers (see page 54) for dipping, or you can use fresh veggies. This is another dish you will be asked to make again and again by family and friends.

Ingredients:

1 can artichokes
3-4 c fresh spinach
1 small onion, diced
4 garlic cloves, minced
1 c Go Veggie cream cheese
⅔ c Vegenaise™ mayo
½ c nutritional yeast
Juice of 1 lemon
Salt and pepper to taste

Directions:

Sauté onion and garlic over medium heat in 1-2 T olive oil until onion turns translucent, about 2 minutes.
Add the artichokes, cream cheese, mayo, nutritional yeast, lemon, and salt and pepper until well combined. Simmer for 5 minutes.
Add the fresh spinach and simmer for 3 minutes until slightly wilted.

Snacks, Appetizers, and Side Dishes

Avocado Chips

Yes, you read that right, avocado CHIPS! Chips are forbidden on keto but these babies will definitely help satisfy that craving if you have it. But, I'll be honest...they are not super crunchy. They are "crispy." The key will be your oven, the cook time and the temp. I've had to play around with the oven to get it at the right crispness I like. They probably won't last long...they never do in my house, but if you do have leftovers keep them in a Ziploc bag in the fridge.

Ingredients:

2 large ripe avocados
1½ c freshly grated vegan parmesan cheese
1 T lemon juice
1 tsp garlic powder
1 tsp Italian seasoning
Pink sea salt and ground pepper to taste

Directions:

Heat oven to 425°. Mix all ingredients in a bowl with a fork and dollop on parchment paper. Bake for 10-15 minutes or longer, depending on how crispy you want them.

Clean Keto
Nooch Crackers

Sometimes you want a real "crunch" that's not coming from a veggie; it's so hard to find vegan/keto crackers in the stores. Trust me, I've looked! They are either vegan or gluten free but never all of the above, but these babies sure are and they satisfy my need for a dipping cracker perfectly. I make them when I make my spinach and artichoke dip, or the tomato and basil fat bombs. No one knows they are so healthy, but everybody loves them.

Ingredients:

1 T Golden Flaxseed Meal
3 T water
1¾ c almond meal (or almond flour)
¼ c nutritional yeast
½ tsp pink sea salt
1 T coconut oil, melted
2 T lemon juice
Kosher or large-flake salt garnish

Directions:

Preheat oven to 425°. In a small bowl, combine flaxseed meal and water and set aside.
Combine almond meal, nutritional yeast, and salt in a large bowl.
Add coconut oil, lemon juice and flaxseed meal mixture.
Mix until a dough forms.
Transfer dough to a piece of parchment paper and cover with a second piece of parchment paper. Roll dough to $1/16$ inch thickness.
Remove top sheet of parchment paper and transfer to a baking sheet. Cut into ½-inch squares. Dock each cracker with a fork and sprinkle generously with pink sea salt.
Bake until deep golden color, about 25 minutes.
Makes about 50 crackers.

Snacks, Appetizers, and Side Dishes

Sowder Slaw

I wanted to include this recipe in my book for several reasons. First of all, the lady who shared it with me is a dear, dear friend and mentor of mine. From the moment I first heard her speak at an event in 2010, to the many years of growing our friendship together, she has always been a positive role model in my life and shown me how to dream big more than anyone else! I've had her famous Sowder Cheese Slaw at her beautiful home more times than I can count…remember, I used to be addicted to cheese, so this was the first dish I went to at her parties. Pam Sowder has been making this slaw for many, many years and has perfected it. As you can see, it's not vegan per the recipe (and I enjoyed it for so many years as it was). I am sure that you too will enjoy it if you are not vegan—that's why I have included her exact recipe. I am also sharing my vegan version that I make as a dip for my Nooch Crackers—guilt free! The option is yours. Thank you, Pam, for allowing me to add this to my cookbook and share with all the world. I love you to the moon and back, my friend!

Ingredients:

3-5 bags of Sargento Shredded Swiss Cheese (Artisan Blends)
1 bag of Sargento Shredded Parmesan Cheese (Artisan Blends)
1-2 T red onion, finely chopped
½ c pickled mild banana peppers, chopped
½ c pickled jalapeño peppers (use a good quality), chopped
Duke's mayonnaise (several Tablespoons but don't overdo it)

Directions:

Blend all the ingredients in a long, rectangular Tupperware-style container with a large fork.
Add small amounts of the Duke's mayo as you go (you don't want it dripping with mayo).
Add more banana peppers or jalapeño depending on if you like it HOT!
I like to dip the slaw onto blue corn chips, but you can put on your favorite cracker, too.
It is great to make a day ahead of time, so put the lid on it and let it sit. Enjoy!

Clean Keto
Vegan Slaw

Ingredients:

5 packages of Daiya brand Swiss Style Cheese, shredded
2 containers of Follow Your Heart shredded parmesan cheese
1-2 T red onion, finely chopped
½ c pickled mild banana peppers, chopped
½ c pickled jalapeño peppers (use a good quality), chopped
Vegenaise™ mayonnaise (several Tablespoons but don't overdo it)

Directions are the same as the original recipe, above.

Enjoy!

Roasted Veggies with Avocado Dressing

This dish will be a hit anywhere you take it...especially in your own home. It's so easy and so versatile. You can use any veggies you have on hand. I make this a lot when I look in my fridge and find one or two pieces of a veggie left over. Maybe one red pepper or just a small amount of broccoli, add an onion and some zucchini and you have an entire tray of roasted veggies. But, this avocado "dressing" is what's really going to WOW your guests! It's creamy and healthy...our neighbor fell in love with it after his first try and, I kid you not, EVERY SINGLE time I see him he asks about this dressing. He's OBSESSED!

Ingredients:

2-4 T oregano
¼-½ c olive oil
Pink sea salt and pepper to taste (the more the better on these veggies)
Fresh veggies of choice (I use onions, peppers, zucchini, cauliflower and/or broccoli)

Directions:

Heat oven to 425°.
Chop all veggies and put on an aluminum foil-lined baking sheet.
Cover with olive oil, salt, pepper and oregano.
Bake 20 minutes and stir veggies.
Bake an additional 15-20 minutes if needed.

Snacks, Appetizers, and Side Dishes

Avocado Dressing

Ingredients:

2 avocados
¼ c olive or avocado oil
1-2 cloves garlic
Juice of 1 lemon

Directions:

Add all ingredients and mix in a NutriBullet® until creamy, not runny.

Desserts and Fat Bombs

Now wait a minute! How can there be desserts when I am basically eating the cleanest I've ever eaten in my entire life? I am gluten free, dairy free, sugar free, and vegan. I mean, what's left? Ice? Well, before you think those sweet treats are gone forever, think again. This section will blow your mind with how healthy these little morsels of amazingness are. Sometimes I find myself eating them for a meal. YES! Guilty! I mean, who wouldn't love a cold glass of unsweetened almond milk with zucchini brownies for dinner? I know I do…and I enjoy every one, guilt free!

Clean Keto
Chocolate Almond Butter Cups

Have you ever had a Cadbury egg? They were always my favorite candy at Easter. Even into adulthood (until I had kids) my mom would do an Easter basket for me. It was filled with Cadbury eggs and usually something really cool I'd been wanting like a new bracelet or a Starbucks™ gift card. You know, back before Amazon, when you could just order it and have it delivered the same day. Well, these chocolate almond butter cups taste as close to Cadbury eggs as anything I've found. The only problem is, I eat them all! But guess what? It's totally fine to eat them all. They are healthy fats.

Ingredients:

1 c Enjoy Life or Lilly's dark chocolate chips
½ c almond butter, room temperature
¼ c coconut oil, room temperature
¼ c vegan butter (Earth Balance), softened
2 T coconut cream (or more as needed)

Directions:

Melt together chocolate chips and coconut cream. Drop a spoonful of melted chocolate mixture into mold and tilt to cover bottom and sides (do not grease molds).
After entire mold is filled with coated sections, pop into the freezer to set, roughly 15 minutes. (I use a 24-section, silicone mini-muffin tray.)
While the molds cool, whip together almond butter, coconut oil and butter.
Remove hardened molds from freezer and plop a spoonful of the almond butter mixture into the centers of each one and smooth it out so it has a flat surface.
Top those with a spoonful of the remaining chocolate and pop them back in the freezer for at least a half hour.
Enjoy!
These are best served cold. Store in fridge.

Blackberry Macadamia Nut Cheesecake Fat Bombs

Where are all my cheesecake lovers? I made this one for my hubby and he fell in love. He is obsessed with cheesecake and it's really hard to find one that beats my mom's. She actually makes a cheesecake from scratch that takes two full days to produce. I tell her all the time she could sell it for $10 a slice, it's that good. These cheesecake fat bombs aren't "that good" but they will definitely satisfy that craving for really good cheesecake. I know my hubby is happy when they are in the fridge!

Ingredients:

2 oz. macadamia nuts
4 oz. softened cream cheese (Go Veggie brand is vegan)
1 c blackberries
1 c coconut oil
1 c coconut butter
½ tsp vanilla
½ tsp lemon juice
¼ c Swerve sweetener or monk fruit

Directions:

Crush macadamia nuts and press into small baking dish; bake at 425° for 7 minutes.
Spread cream cheese over crust.
Mix blackberries, coconut oil, lemon juice, and Swerve.
Pour over crust and freeze for 30 minutes. Store in fridge.
Enjoy these little slices of heaven.

Clean Keto
Chocolate Almond Butter Fat Bombs

Want a quick, easy, and super chocolaty treat? That's what these babies are. They literally take 5 minutes to prepare and 10 minutes in the freezer and you are eating a piece of chocolate heaven. I like to mix it up and put a pecan on top sometimes while other times I'll add a walnut. But, my latest crave is adding Lilly's dark chocolate chips to the batter before I freeze them. So yummy! (Remember, I am a chocoholic.)

Ingredients:

¼ c fresh almond butter
¼ c coconut oil
2 T cacao powder
¼ c Monkfruit sweetener

Directions:

Mix all ingredients and drop into 24-section silicone mini-muffin tray. Freeze for 10 minutes. Keep stored in the fridge.

Chocolate Chip Cookie Dough Fat Bombs

Well, here they are. The mac daddy of FAT BOMBS! These chocolate chip cookie dough fat bombs taste identical to REAL cookie dough. I don't totally understand because I don't bake... especially from scratch, but as I've mentioned, my mom does and these taste just like licking the beater after she made the chocolate chip cookie dough. MIND BLOWN on this one for sure!

Ingredients:

8 oz. Go Veggie cream cheese, softened
½ c Earth Balance butter, softened
½ c fresh almond butter
¼ c Swerve sweetener
½ c Enjoy Life or Lilly's dark chocolate chips

Directions:

In a mixing bowl, using an electric mixer, mix all ingredients excluding chocolate chips until well combined.
Refrigerate mixture for 30 minutes.
Fold in chocolate chips, drop into cookie-size bites and freeze for 30 minutes. Or, if you're as crazy about this as I am, just go ahead and eat 3-4 spoonfuls right out of the bowl! You won't regret it.

Clean Keto
Red, White, and Blue Cheesecake Fat Bombs

These are a super fun 4th of July treat, but absolutely can be made any time of the year when you need a sweet treat. These do take a little longer to prepare than most fat bombs because they're done in layers, but it's worth it for how they look and taste. So yummy!

Ingredients:

For Strawberry Base:
6-8 strawberries
8 oz. Go Veggie cream cheese
1 T water
Freeze for 15-30 min
For Cheesecake Middle Layer:
8 oz. Go Veggie cream cheese
½ c butter melted
1 T monk fruit or Swerve sweetener
1 T vanilla extract
¼ c coconut oil
Freeze for 15-30 minutes
For Blueberry Top Layer:
½ c coconut oil
1 container blueberries
1 T Swerve sweetener or monk fruit

Directions:

Mix all ingredients for strawberry base and put in silicon 12-section muffin tray, freeze 15-30 minutes.
In a medium-sized mixing bowl, add the butter and cream cheese and mix with an electric mixer until combined.
Add the vanilla extract, Swerve, and coconut oil, mix again until combined.
Grab your silicon cupcake tray from the freezer and smooth cheesecake on top of base layer.
Freeze for 15-30 minutes.
Mix all ingredients for the blueberry top layer and smooth the blueberry top layer flat with a small teaspoon.
Place in freezer for up to 4 hours until all ingredients are hard.
They will pop out easily using a silicon muffin tray and look beautiful.

Zucchini Brownies

Yes, I know, how can these be food? I mean, zucchini and chocolate don't just go hand in hand. Or do they? Think about zucchini bread. Yum! I used to eat that like crazy as a kid. My mom would make it fresh all summer long so I was very used it. But, if you're not so sure, just put your reservations aside for a minute and I promise you won't regret it. The zucchini is grated so you won't even know it's in there, and all you will get are super chocolatey fudge brownies that you could eat for dinner if you wanted to. Speaking from experience! I even took these to my gym for a special treat to share. Every single brownie was devoured, so you know they are yummy!

Ingredients:

2 c grated zucchini
1 c almond butter or tahini
½ c raw cacao powder or more if you love chocolate like I do
1 flax or flax/chia egg (1 T of flax or flax chia blend mixed with 3 T water, mixed and allow to congeal for 5 minutes)
¼-½ c Golden monk fruit
1 tsp baking soda
½ tsp of Himalayan salt
½ c Lilly's dark chocolate chips + ¼ c for sprinkling on top

Directions:

Preheat your oven to 425°.
Coat your 9 x 9-inch pan with olive oil.
Grate your zucchini and place it in a clean dish towel.
Wrap the towel tightly around the zucchini and squeeze all of the water out.
The recipe works best the drier the zucchini is.
Add all ingredients except chocolate chips into a mixing bowl.
With a wooden spoon, blend thoroughly.
Mix in chocolate chips by hand.
Spoon mixture into your pan and add extra chocolate chips on top.
Bake for 15-20 minutes.
Enjoy immediately with a cold glass of unsweetened almond milk.

Clean Keto
Avocado Pudding

You know what I love about this rich and creamy recipe? You would never know there is avocado in it if I didn't tell you. I find that loving avocado is about 50/50 in the world of keto. Some people eat them like apples and other people, like ME, want them disguised in the bowl. Whether it's in desserts or in fresh guac or hummus, I like to have other stuff mixed with mine. Be sure to add extra monk fruit if you have a sweet tooth like I do.

Ingredients:

1 avocado
¼ c cacao powder
1 T monk fruit or more to taste
½ tsp vanilla
1 tsp salt

Directions:

Mix with spoon in a bowl and enjoy!

Desserts and Fat Bombs

One-Minute Cinnamon Roll Mug Cake

Much like the blueberry muffin dessert, this cinnamon roll cake is super quick, easy, and yummy. But I will tell you, the type of protein powder you use will make a difference in how they taste. My hubby loves our plant-based protein Creamy Vanilla It Works! Shake™ and drinks one daily with Keto Coffee™ in it, so these are totally amazing to him. I, on the other hand, only like the Creamy Vanilla It Works! Shake™ if I've added a scoop of Keto Creamer and a scoop of lemon Ketones™. This mug cake is an incredible dessert that's super low in carbs and totally vegan (if using vegan protein powder).

Ingredients:

1 scoop Creamy Vanilla It Works! Shake™ protein powder
½ tsp baking powder
1 T coconut flour
½ tsp cinnamon or more to taste
1 T monk fruit
¼ c unsweetened almond milk
¼ tsp vanilla extract

Directions:

Stir all ingredients together in a mug and pop in the microwave for 1 min, 30 sec. Or, bake at 425° in oven for 10 minutes.

Clean Keto
Snickerdoodle Fat Bombs

In the world of fat bombs, this one is the bomb.com for sure! It just amazes me how these taste JUST LIKE the snickerdoodle cookie batter that my mom used to make growing up. That was always my favorite cookie right next to chocolate chip (pictured below, too, along with the Chocolate Almond Butter Fat Bombs on page 62), so when I first saw this recipe I thought for sure there was no way it could compare; but, it has far exceeded my expectations. Everyone who has tried them totally agrees. I often take these to the gym as a special treat for my buddies and there are never any left over.

Ingredients:

8 oz. Go Veggie cream cheese
½ c Earth Balance vegan butter
½ c fresh almond butter
⅓ c monk fruit or Swerve sweetener
1 tsp cinnamon
1 tsp vanilla extract
For the Coating:
3 T golden monk fruit
1 tsp cinnamon
Dash of sea salt

Directions:

Mix all ingredients together with an electric mixer in a bowl and place in the fridge for 30 minutes.
Mix the coating ingredients in a small dish and set aside.
Remove the chilled dough and form into small balls.
Dip each one into the coating, turning over to coat well.
Place on lined pan in freezer.
When you are ready for one, just remove from freezer and let it thaw for one minute (if you can wait that long!)

Pumpkin Pie Fat Bombs

At the writing of this cookbook it's technically the start of fall, the autumnal equinox, and, well, my birthday! And, being a girl who grew up in the Midwest, I remember the temperatures always started to drop this time of year and the smell of pumpkins began to fill the country roads that had become lined with gold and red-leafed trees. Fast forward 40 years and I am living in paradise—South Florida—so fall is a thing of the past. Of course, people start to decorate with wreaths and pumpkins and fall yard signs, but it's still 95 degrees out and smells nothing like fall yet. Nonetheless, my internal clock screams *pumpkin pie!* and that's just what this fat bomb is. Actually, I am calling it a pumpkin pie tart because it does have the solid consistency like most fat bombs, but it is oh-so-yummy and totally satisfies the need for pumpkin in my life at this time of year!

Ingredients:

½ c pumpkin puree
¼ c coconut butter
½ c coconut oil
¼ c monk fruit
2 tsp pumpkin pie spice
½ c pecans, toasted

Directions:

Melt your coconut butter until it's soft and easier to work with.
Combine the pumpkin puree, coconut butter, and coconut oil in a mixing bowl and stir until combined. Add the monk fruit.
Add the pumpkin pie spice as well. If you don't have pumpkin pie spice, just adding cinnamon will do, about 2 teaspoons.
Once your fat bomb batter is combined, add it into your 12-section silicon muffin tray.
Lastly, toast up some chopped pecans and sprinkle them on top.
Place in fridge for 20-30 minutes and enjoy.

How to Make It All Work for YOU

Where am I Supposed to Start?

If you're considering transitioning to a plant-based diet, take baby steps; you don't have to make the change overnight. (Attempting something too drastic is a set-up to fail.) Try having just one or two big meals a week and work from there. Add new vegan foods to your diet and slowly remove animal-based foods. If you make the transition at your own pace, it will be easier to stick with it in the long run, but don't be too hard on yourself if you make mistakes. Being vegan isn't about being perfect, it's about living a healthier, more compassionate life. As long as you keep that in mind, you'll be fine. Along your journey, remember to tell yourself, "progress, not perfection" is what there is to celebrate.

Right Where You Are is the Perfect Place to Start

Unless you are already "there," you do not need to begin with veganism. To help get you started, I created a 14-day meal plan which is primarily animal-based but sprinkles in a variety of plant-based options. I know when I started I still had cravings for cheese, eggs, and my favorite seafood. As you begin using this cookbook, I urge you to look over the next three sections on setting up your kitchen, helpful ingredients to stock, and useful kitchen tools to help you prepare. The key to getting more comfortable with healthy cooking is to dive right in rather than shun away from an ingredient you haven't heard of. Embrace it. If there's a technique you have never tried, give it a whirl. And, if you make a mistake, it's okay! Mistakes are the best way for you to learn and adapt to a new way of cooking. I've googled and you-tubed my way through this journey, so don't stress. You will get the hang of it.

Before I give you a time-saving shopping list I've developed, I want to share with you something you must stop and think about; is your kitchen your health partner, or your worst influence? A nutrition scientist and dietitian I know teaches "Purpose-Driven Kitchen" principles and these will help you as you set yourself up for success. Here is what Barbara shares with us:

The Purpose-Driven Kitchen

I. THE ENVIRONMENTAL INFLUENCE

Every room in your home has a purpose.

If your home is a reflection of who you are, then your kitchen is a reflection of the way you eat and the way you feel about food.

People are, to one degree or another, a product of their environment.

When you take personal responsibility for your environment, and **cause** it to be one that supports good health, you will find yourself enjoying better health.

How to Make It All Work for YOU

One key to success in your goal of good health is to surround yourself with the tools that make your success more likely. By tools we mean consciously designed space, an inventory of healthy recipes and foods, and a system for maintaining good habits (such as a meal-planning system.)

What is the purpose of your kitchen?

Generally, the purpose of the kitchen is to provide a convenient, clean space to store and prepare food. A kitchen's 'Higher Purpose' is to be a Center of Nourishment.

What are 3 Common Mistakes that Turn Your Kitchen Against You?

1. Inventory inconsistent with new healthy lifestyle.
2. Poor choices are more convenient than good choices.
3. Clutter makes the purpose of the kitchen unclear.

Instead…make your kitchen your Wellness Partner by helping you

- Prevent temptations
- Promote convenience of healthy choices
- Purchase wisely

What **needs to change** in your current kitchen lay-out or contents to have it be more of a Wellness Partner for you?

"If you're saying something is important in your life but you aren't spending time on it, then change what you say your values are, or the way you spend your time." Ken Blanchard, PhD, author *"The One Minute Manager"*

II. ORGANIZED FOR HEALTH SUCCESS

Clutter is an obstacle to your intentions. It impedes your ability to find things, use things, appreciate things, and to leverage the space and resources you have to build a healthy and rewarding life.

Simplify by removing what you never use or no longer want to have in your space.

Organize by having a place designated for everything, and everything in its place.

A kitchen make-over will require intention, time, and focus.

FOCUS: Follow One Course Until Successful

Clean Keto

III. HEALTHFUL INVENTORY

Example:

- ✓ Unsweetened almond milk
- ✓ Golden monk fruit sweetener
- ✓ Coconut oil
- ✓ Olive oil
- ✓ Pink Himalayan sea salt
- ✓ Frozen berries
- ✓ Olive oil
- ✓ Onions
- ✓ Walnuts
- ✓ Tofu

You will be creating your own Healthy Staples Checklist.

That way you will always have what supports you on hand.

What are some items you would like to see in these areas?

- Pantry
- Spices and seasonings
- Freezer
- Other areas (car, purse, fridge at work, etc.)
- Snack basket or shelf
- Refrigerator
- Supplies

IV. MEAL PLANNING

Creating a *system* is the perfect solution for any routine task.

A system has four elements:

1. Name.
2. Designated location and set-up of items needed.
3. Frequency defined.
4. Procedure.

Some of the benefits to using such a system for planning a week's worth of meals include:

- Insures healthy choices are always available.
- Takes stress out of shopping because you have your trustworthy list with you.
- Saves money by only buying what you don't have, and will actually use.
- Helps you feel ready for the week ahead, affirms your control.

How to Make It All Work for YOU

- Saves time by significantly reducing the number of trips to the grocery store.
- Saves money because you never have to go out to eat just because there's nothing at home, or nothing planned.
- Allows you to make healthy choices for your family's meals ahead of time, when you are focused on healthy, yet "favorite" meals.
- Teaches family how to think in terms of complete, healthy, enjoyable meals. Adding a new Favorite Meal is something everyone can help with.
- Makes it easy for someone else to take over preparing dinner if you are not home.
- Gives you a system you can use if you are going to spend a week at a vacation house.

Me with our son, Trey.

OUR FAVORITE HOME-PREPARED MEALS

List seven complete meals to start your library of Favorite Meals. You can put the name of the main dish and other parts of your complete meal on one side of an index card, and the full recipe with instructions on the back (including amounts, seasonings, etc.). Or, you could use a notes or list app on your phone if that is how you roll. Just make it easy to use, for you.

Add to your library as you go. For some people, involving their family in developing the meal cards is a fun and easy way to get everyone on the same page for healthy, tasty menus.

V. MAINTENANCE

(Keeping Hellish Stuff Out of Your Heavenly Kitchen)

As noted: People are, to one degree or another, a product of their environment.

When you take personal responsibility for your environment, and **cause** it to be one that supports good health, you will find yourself enjoying better health.

Clean Keto

One key to success in your goal of good health is to surround yourself with the tools that make your success more likely. By tools we mean consciously designed space, an inventory of healthy recipes and foods, and a system for maintaining good habits. You can create a kitchen to nourish those habits.

Take a moment to note your next actions toward creating your IDEAL KITCHEN, one that HELPS your HEALTHY LIFESTYLE.

Making Time to Live Your Best Life

So, what do you do when you are "on the go" or if your family doesn't want to eat this ultra-healthy way, or you are super busy with your work and travel? These are the top things people ask me. They tell me they are too busy and work so much and are running their kids all over God's green Earth and don't have time to "meal prep" or eat on the run. They say they don't have time to cook each day just for themselves or they are in their car all day and don't have time to do anything but a drive-thru. Well, let's be completely honest for a minute. We are all as busy as we want to be! We create our days and nights and weeks and months so if we look at them and think that we don't have enough time to eat, and eat properly for our health and well-being, then we need to do a reality check with ourselves and decide what truly matters each and every day.

If someone told you that they would take your children and not give them back until you paid them $1 million dollars, you better believe you would drop everything and focus solely on getting that

How to Make It All Work for YOU

money in record time! Heck, with social media today you could have it in minutes! But, thankfully, this is not that serious...or is it? Only you know what your health looks like. Only you know how you feel on a daily basis. Only you know what you are putting in your mouth each and every day. So, if looking healthy and feeling amazing on the inside and out are priorities for you, then you will definitely make time to fit them in your schedule! I know this because I have been there. I have used, "I am too busy traveling to worry about it;" "I don't like to cook;" "My family doesn't eat this way;" and so on and so on!

What do you do about it? You become intentional—you make a plan and you get prepared. There is no way everyone in your house is going to eat exactly the same things you do. That idea is insane to begin with. If I don't like peas, then why in the world would I think that because my spouse is eating them that I have to as well? If I don't like peas, I am not eating them, plain and simple! He can, of course. But not me. So, let's look at meal time and meal planning in that way. I am not saying that you can't all sit down together as a family and eat a meal together consisting of the same things. I am just saying be open to the possibility that you may be eating certain foods while other people in the family, who have different tastes, are eating *other* foods.

Let's look at eating vegan/keto that way. Some people may not like olives. Great! They don't have to put them on their plate, but you are. No biggie, right? Everyone will be okay not eating the same things, and no one should be forced to eat things that don't taste good to them. Food should be enjoyable, not seem like a source of punishment. Don't you want to enjoy your food, eat things that taste amazing to *you*, and look forward to the next time you have that again? I know I do! I can hear so many of you parents right now…"Well, Johnny has to at least try the foods I make." I am totally fine with him trying them, but if he doesn't like it, please don't force him to eat it, over and over and over again, just because you cooked it. What kind of food associations are being set up with that? Not the healthy ones you want to promote. So, ask your family members for their input once a week, as mentioned earlier in the setting up your conscious, "purpose-driven" kitchen section. Give them ownership, and take some yourself as well. Everyone will be trying new things and finding foods they love…and soon they will start asking for these healthy foods over and over again. Remember—baby steps—but you have to take steps forward each day to a new healthier you.

Clean Keto

If you are on the go a lot like I am, you really need to be prepared so you stay satisfied and focused on your health goals. I always have snacks in my house that I can take with me if I am traveling to and from appointments. I keep pecans, macadamia nuts, and walnuts in my car at all times. I can always snack on those healthy fats that are sure to fill me up fast, even in the car. I keep fat bombs in my freezer at all times so I can grab a quick treat on the way out the door or after a meal if I need to satisfy my sweet tooth. If I am traveling out of town, whether by car or plane, I literally take food with me in my suitcase: Keto Coffee™, Ketones™, shakes, almond butter, nuts, and bars are 100% of the time packed in that suitcase…even before the clothes! You better believe that I will stay happy and full no matter where I am. I even travel with plastic spoons, napkins, and my frother. No one cares, and if they do, I DON'T! I am full, satisfied and staying on target with my goals. Remember, being prepared sets you up for success.

If I am going to be in a different city for a few days, the first thing I do after I grab my rental car is head to the local healthy grocery store. If I am in a house or a hotel, I can always utilize the fridge to keep some healthy veggies and snacks on hand. If I am out and about locally, I will plan a quick stop at one of my local faves to grab a quick healthy lunch on the go and eat it in the car while catching up on emails or social media. Where there is a will, there's a way, and this is you using YOUR willpower over yourself to be prepared and make healthy choices. Your body will thank you for it!

Okay, so some of you are thinking, *well, what about that cheat meal I had? I caved in and ate the burger and fries in the drive-thru.* Well, don't beat yourself up. Drink your Ketones™ and get back in ketosis. Learn from that mistake so you are better prepared next time! Remember, this is a learning process and you are going to make some mistakes. As long as you learn from them and make better choices the next time, it's all good. You can do this. If I can do this, so can you. We all have a life. We all have work or kids or responsibilities. Decide today that you will make living your best life a priority and let's go on this journey together!

My husband, Brent, finds many pleasures in my keto cooking.

Ultimate Vegan/Keto Shopping List

Notes:

Foods marked with an asterisk (*) are a little bit higher in carbs and should be consumed sparingly.

Foods marked with a (p) are good sources of protein.

These foods are commonly available in most supermarkets in the U.S. and Canada

Vegan/Keto Fats:

Nuts:

- Almonds (p)
- Brazil nuts
- Cashews*
- Hazelnuts/filberts
- Macadamia nuts
- Pecans
- Pine nuts*
- Pistachios*
- Walnuts

Seeds:

- Chia seeds
- Flax seeds
- Hemp seeds (p)
- Pumpkin seeds (p)
- Sunflower seeds (p)

Nut and Seed Butters:

- Almond butter (p)
- Coconut butter (also called coconut manna)
- Macadamia nut butter
- Sunflower seed butter
- Tahini
- Walnut butter

Other Whole Food Fat Sources:

- Avocados
- Coconut
- Olives

Clean Keto

Healthy Oils:

- Almond oil
- Avocado oil
- Coconut oil
- Macadamia nut oil
- MCT oil
- Olive oil
- Walnut oil

Low Carb Fruits and Vegetables:

Low Carb Vegetables:

- Artichoke hearts
- Arugula
- Asparagus
- Bell peppers (green are lowest in carbs)
- Beets*

- Bok choy
- Broccoli
- Brussels sprouts*
- Cabbage
- Carrots*
- Cauliflower
- Celery
- Chard
- Collards
- Cucumbers
- Eggplant
- Endive (also called escarole)
- Fennel
- Garlic
- Jicama*
- Kale*
- Kohlrabi (p)
- Lettuce (all types)
- Mushrooms
- Mustard greens
- Okra
- Onion*
- Radishes
- Rhubarb
- Rutabaga*
- Shallots
- Spinach
- Squash – winter type* (butternut, pumpkin, spaghetti)

Ultimate Vegan/Keto Shopping List

- Squash – summer type
- Swiss chard
- Turnips
- Zucchini

Low Carb Fruits:

- Avocado
- Blueberries*
- Coconut
- Cranberries
- Lemon
- Lime
- Olives
- Raspberries
- Strawberries
- Tomatoes
- Watermelon*

Low Carb Vegan Pantry Staples:

- Almond flour
- Baking powder
- Baking soda
- Coconut flour
- Coconut milk (canned, full fat)
- Cacao powder
- Dark chocolate (85% and up is usually super low in sugar, but be sure to check the label. I love Endangered Species brand.)
- Jackfruit (green, canned in brine, not syrup)
- Psyllium husk
- Nutritional yeast
- Vanilla extract (check for sugar!)

Low Carb Vegan Fridge Staples:

- Apple cider vinegar
- Dairy free cheese* (If you must have it, Follow Your Heart has the best flavor.)
- Pickles (dill, or other sugar-free types)
- Micro-greens

- Sauerkraut or vegan kimchi
- Seitan* (p) (if not gluten intolerant)
- Sprouts (all kinds)
- Tempeh (p)
- Tofu (p)
- Tomato paste

Other Vegan/Keto Meal Staples:

- Lots of herbs and spices
- Edamame
- Pasta Zero noodles

Clean Keto

- Shirataki noodles
- Roasted seaweed snacks

Vegan/Keto Sauces and Condiments:

- Chili sauce or hot sauce of choice
- Mustard
- Soy sauce/tamari/coconut aminos
- Tomato sauce (check labels carefully for sugar!)
- Vinegar – balsamic, rice wine, white wine
- Wasabi paste (check label!)

Vegan/Keto Freezer Items:

- Beyond Meat meat substitutes
- Cauliflower rice
- Gardein meatless products (some are okay but not all, so check labels to be sure there is no sugar added)
- Frozen vegetables (anything from the above list)
- Frozen berries

Egg-Free, Dairy-Free Keto Protein Powders and Bars:

- It Works!™ vegan protein powder (chocolate or vanilla)
- Julian Bakery Pegan Bars (Ginger Snap ones are my favorite)

I hope you find this list useful. I like to keep a printout in my reusable shopping bags, so it's always with me when I go to the grocery store. Even though I've mostly got this down now, sometimes just referencing my handy-dandy vegan/keto shopping list can mean I don't forget to buy ingredients I need. I get too excited sometimes, and buy things I don't need, while completely forgetting what I came there for! Another way to keep your list handy is to have it on your phone, since we almost always have our phone attached to us.

14-Day Keto Meal Plan

Every Day

Drink ½ your body weight in OUNCES of water EVERY DAY. If you weigh 150 pounds, that's 75 oz. per day. If you consume alcohol or caffeinated drinks, you need to drink at least an extra 16 oz. of water per drink. But while on the keto plan, of course, you won't be drinking much of those, will you?

Consume Ketones™ every morning to keep your electrolytes in balance and to avoid "keto flu," which is what some people call symptoms like headaches, nausea, body aches and stomach aches, which can occur if you do not drink enough water plus electrolytes. I use the It Works! Lemon Ketones™, mixed in 12 oz. iced water, and drink it on the way to the gym.

Fast at least 12 hours; 16 hours for the best results and be sure to see my section on intermittent fasting on pages 5 and 6.

Note: This plan is NOT VEGAN, in order to make it easier to try KETO first…maybe vegan later. Of course vegans can use this plan by substituting your favorite proteins for meat.

Day 1

It Works! Ketones™ upon rising, mixed in 12 oz. water.

30 minutes-1 hour later, Keto Coffee™ mixed in 8-10 oz. water.

So I have my lemon Ketones™ before the gym, and my Keto Coffee™ after.

Optional Breakfast:

Tomato and Avocado Omelet

½ avocado
½ roma tomato
1 T chopped basil
2 eggs
½ T olive oil

Directions: Heat oil in skillet. Whisk eggs with 2 T water and salt and pepper. Add eggs to skillet on medium heat for 3 minutes. Layer with avocado and tomatoes. Fold and top with fresh basil.

Clean Keto

Lunch:

Super Simple Salami Salad

3 T sour cream
2 tsp Dijon mustard
¼ c cherry tomatoes
⅛ red onion
2 hard-boiled eggs
2 oz. salami
1¼ c arugula

Mix together sour cream, mustard, 1 T water, salt and pepper to taste. Whisk in more water if you want your dressing thinner. Cut tomatoes, peel and slice onion, chop hard boiled eggs and salami. Combine all together in a bowl with arugula. Dollop with dressing to coat.

Snack:

½ c macadamia nuts

Dinner:

Garlic Butter Tilapia with Asparagus and Tomatoes

1 T butter
1 tsp minced garlic
¼ lemon
¼ tsp Italian seasoning
6 oz. asparagus
½ c cherry tomatoes
1 T olive oil
6 oz. tilapia

Directions: Preheat oven to 425°. Line a baking sheet with foil. Melt butter in a small bowl and whisk in garlic, lemon juice, and Italian seasoning. Trim bottom, tough ends off asparagus and place the spears on one side of the baking sheet. Add cherry tomatoes and drizzle both with olive oil. Season with salt and pepper. Add tilapia to the vegetables and brush with ½ the butter mixture. Place in oven and cook 12-15 minutes until fish flakes easily with a fork. Enjoy tilapia with remaining butter sauce for dipping. Feel free to change the fish.

Snack:

1-2 Almond Butter/Chocolate Fat Bombs

¼ c almond butter
¼ c unrefined coconut oil
2 T cacao powder
¼ c erythritol (I use powdered Swerve)

Directions: Mix together almond butter and coconut oil in a medium bowl. Microwave for 30-45 seconds. Stir until smooth. Stir in erythritol and cacao powder. Pour into silicone molds and refrigerate until firm.

Day 2

It Works! Ketones™ upon rising, mixed in 12 oz. water; or, Keto Go before a morning workout

30 minutes-1 hour later, Keto Coffee™ mixed in 8-10 oz. water, or your coffee of choice with Keto Creamer added

Optional Breakfast:

Ham, Egg and Spinach Roll-Ups

½ tomato
1 tsp olive oil
1 c spinach
2 eggs
2 slices ham (not too thinly sliced)

Directions: Dice tomatoes. Place skillet on medium-high heat and add olive oil and spinach for 1 minute. Lightly beat egg in a small bowl with a pinch of salt and add egg to pan, stirring gently until it starts to set. Add tomato and remove from the heat. Add pepper to taste. Place ham on flat surface and spoon egg mixture into the center of each, like a burrito, and fold ham over the filling. Place wraps back in the pan for 30 seconds on each side until ham is lightly browned.

Clean Keto

Lunch:

It Works!™ Shake

Add creamer and/or lemon Ketones™ if desired

Snack:

20 olives (can be stuffed with cheese, etc.)

Dinner:

Keto Cobb Salad with Ranch Dressing

2 eggs
5 oz. bacon
½ rotisserie chicken

2 oz. blue cheese
1 avocado
1 tomato

½ lb. iceberg lettuce
1 T fresh chives (optional)
Salt and ground black pepper

Easy Ranch Dressing:

3 T mayonnaise
½-1 T ranch seasoning
2-3 T water
Salt and ground black pepper

Directions: Start by preparing the dressing. Combine mayonnaise, ranch seasoning and water. Add salt and pepper, set aside.
Place the eggs in boiling water for 8-10 minutes. Cool in ice water for easier peeling. Chop them roughly.
Fry bacon in a hot, dry skillet until crispy. Cut grilled chicken in smaller pieces and chop up vegetables. If using raw chicken, fry in the bacon fat, add salt and pepper to taste. Crumble the blue cheese. Distribute everything on a bed of shredded lettuce. Add salt and pepper.
Drizzle with dressing and top with finely chopped chives

Snack:

Lemon Fat Bombs

7 oz. coconut butter, softened
¼ c extra-virgin coconut oil, softened
1-2 T organic lemon zest or lemon extract (1-2 tsp), depending on your palate
15-20 drops stevia extract (clear or lemon)
Pinch of pink Himalayan salt

Clean Keto

Day 3

Ketones™ upon rising, mixed in 12 oz. water; or, Keto Go before a morning workout

30 minutes-1 hour later, Keto Coffee™ mixed in 8-10 oz. hot or cold water

Optional Breakfast:

Keto Cinnamon Swirl Bread

4 eggs, separated
¼ tsp cream of tarter
2 T butter, melted
2 T butter, softened
1 tsp vanilla extract
3 oz. cream cheese, softened

Liquid stevia to taste (I use about 12 drops)
1 tsp baking powder
1 c almond flour
1½ tsp cinnamon, divided
¼ c erythritol (I prefer confectioners)

Directions: Preheat the oven to 350° and prepare a 9 x 5-inch loaf pan with non-stick spray. Separate the egg whites and yolks into 2 large bowls. Add the cream of tartar to the egg whites and beat with an electric mixer until soft peaks form. Set aside. Add melted butter, vanilla extract, cream cheese, and stevia to the egg yolks. Mix until well combined. Then add ½ tsp of cinnamon, baking powder, and almond flour, stirring until well combined. In a small bowl, combine the softened butter, erythritol, and the remaining 1 tsp of cinnamon. Stir to combine and set aside. Fold the egg whites into the egg yolk mixture. This may take a few minutes as the egg yolk mixture may be fairly thick. Pour half of the egg mixture into the prepared loaf pan. Evenly top with the cinnamon and butter mixture. Then add the remaining egg mixture, ensuring that the mixture has been spread to the edges of the pan. Using a butter knife, make swirls into the bread, keeping the knife vertical to prevent too much mixing between the layers. Bake for 30-40 minutes, or until the top is golden.

Lunch:

It Works! Shake™

Add creamer or lemon Ketones™ if desired to taste like a lemon pound cake

Snack:

Smarter Ants on a Log

¼ c almond butter with celery sticks

Dinner:

Avocado Kale Salad

1 bunch kale (de-stemmed and cut into bite-sized pieces)
2 T red onion, diced
2 T red peppers, diced
2 T green onions, sliced short
2 T olive oil
2 T lemon juice
1 avocado (remove pit and squeeze out of skin)
1 pinch salt
2 plum tomatoes, chopped

Directions: Place all ingredients except tomatoes in a medium-large mixing bowl. Gently mix and massage the avocado into the kale, almost like kneading meatloaf. (I find that hands are the best tool for this combining process—disposable gloves optional.) Continue until kale is a dark glistening green, about 3 minutes. Lightly toss in tomatoes and serve. Add meat of your choice if you desire.

Clean Keto

Day 4

Ketones™ upon rising, mixed in 12 oz. water

30 minutes-1 hour later, Keto Coffee™ mixed in 8-10 oz. water

Lunch:

It Works! Shake™ (Creamy Vanilla or Rich Chocolate)

Add almond butter and/or vegan dark chocolate chips

Dinner:

Keto Paleo Chicken Enchilada Boats

2 lbs. boneless skinless chicken thighs
16 fl. oz. Kettle & Fire Chicken Bone Broth
½ c tomato sauce
1 small yellow onion, diced
1 small yellow bell pepper, diced
3 T avocado oil
2 tsp chili powder
1 tsp paprika
1 tsp garlic powder
½ tsp ground cumin
¼ tsp ground cayenne
¼ tsp gray sea salt
3 medium zucchinis, sliced in half lengthwise
Optional: 1 c shredded dairy-free or regular cheese, 1 batch vegan sour cream, 1 tomato, diced or handful fresh cilantro, diced

Directions: Place chicken thighs and bone broth in a stock pot or your Instant Pot® Pressure Cooker. If using a stock pot, cover and bring to a boil on high heat. Reduce heat and simmer for 2 hours. If using an Instant Pot® Pressure Cooker, set to high pressure for 35 minutes.
Preheat oven to 375°.
Strain the bone broth from the chicken and shred the chicken in the pot or pressure cooker.
Add the tomato sauce, diced onion, diced bell pepper, avocado oil, chili powder, paprika, garlic powder, ground cumin, ground cayenne, and salt. Stir to coat.

Scoop out the insides from the zucchini pieces, leaving about ¼-inch thickness on all sides. Place the zucchini pieces scoop side up on a cookie sheet.

Divide the chicken mixture between the zucchini pieces. Then, cover in cheese if using. Transfer the cookie sheet to the preheated oven and bake for 25-30 minutes, until cheese has melted and zucchini is fork-tender.

Remove from the oven and top with sour cream, tomato, and cilantro.

Snack:

1-2 Fat Bombs

Day 5

Ketones™ upon rising, mixed in 12 oz. water

30 minutes-1 hour later, Keto Coffee™ mixed in 8-10 oz. water

Optional Breakfast:

Scrambled eggs with bacon

Lunch:

Tofu and Green Beans with Homemade Ranch Dressing

¼ c olive oil
1 block extra firm tofu
¼ c onion
1 c green beans
Pink sea salt and pepper to taste

Dressing:

½ c low carb mayo
1 tsp garlic powder
1 T fresh dill

Clean Keto

Directions: Heat the skillet on high heat with the olive oil. Sauté the chopped onions. Add the tofu after cutting it into rectangle strips. Add pink sea salt and pepper to taste. Brown for 5 minutes on each side at high heat. Add the green beans and cook, reducing the heat to medium-high for 10 minutes. For the dressing, put all ingredients in a NutriBullet® or the like to blend. Will keep in the fridge for up to a week.

Snack:

¼ c sunflower butter with veggies

Dinner:

Easy Pork Stir Fry Recipe with Vegetables (Low Carb)

¾ pound pork loin, cut into thin strips
2 T avocado or olive oil (divided)
1 T minced fresh ginger
1 tsp minced garlic
12 oz. broccoli florets
1 red bell pepper, cut into strips
1 bunch green onions (scallions), cut into 2-inch pieces
2 T tamari soy sauce (or coconut aminos)
1 T extra dry sherry
1½ T Sukrin:1 (or Swerve Granulated) (or sugar or coconut sugar)
1 tsp cornstarch (or arrowroot)
1 tsp sesame oil
Optional Ingredients:
Red pepper flakes
Sesame seeds

Directions: Mince or press a peeled clove of garlic. Cut a 1-inch piece of ginger and peel the thin skin with a spoon. Mince the ginger and add it to the garlic. Cut the pork loin into thin strips and mix with 1 T oil, the ginger and garlic.
Remove seeds and core and cut the red bell pepper into strips and place into the bottom of a medium bowl. Cut the green onions (scallions) into 2-inch pieces, including some of the green stems, and add them to the bowl. Cut the broccoli florets into large bite-sized pieces, layering them on top.
Add the sweetener and cornstarch (arrowroot) to a small bowl and mix together. Stir in the tamari

soy sauce, dry sherry and sesame oil.

Place the wok over high heat. It's ready when a drop of water skips across the surface. Add 1 T of oil and quickly tilt the wok to coat all surfaces. Pour out the remaining oil. Place the wok back onto the heat and begin adding the pork to the sides and bottom of the pan. Leave the pork undisturbed until it has cooked half way through; the bottom half will turn white. Stir the pork and cook until it is almost cooked through. Remove from the pan to the serving bowl.

Dump the bowl of vegetables into the wok with the broccoli in the bottom. Cover with a lid and cook for 1 minute. Stir the vegetables and add the pork and any juices back to the pan. Stir the pork and vegetables together. Stir the stir fry sauce and pour it over the pork and vegetables. Push the pork stir fry to the sides and let the sauce boil at the bottom of the wok, stirring occasionally for several seconds until the sauce thickens.

If you would like the sauce a little thicker, remove the stir-fried pork and vegetables and place into the serving bowl, letting the sauce cook a little longer. Pour the sauce over the stir fry when it reaches your desired level of thickness. Ready to enjoy!

Snack:

½ c macadamia nuts

Day 6

Ketones™ upon rising, mixed in 12 oz. water

30 minutes-1 hour later, Keto Coffee™ mixed in 8-10 oz. water

Lunch:

It Works! Shake™ (Creamy Vanilla or Rich Chocolate)

Add berries of choice with unsweetened almond milk

Snack:

20 stuffed olives of choice

Dinner:

Easy Four Cheese Pesto Zoodles

8 oz. mascarpone cheese
¼ c grated parmesan cheese
¼ c grated Romano cheese
½ tsp kosher salt
¼ tsp ground black pepper
⅛ tsp ground nutmeg
¼ c basil pesto (store-bought or homemade)
8 c raw zucchini noodles (aka. spiral cut zucchini)
1 c grated mozzarella cheese

Directions: Preheat the oven to 400°. Microwave the zucchini noodles uncovered, on high, for 3 minutes. Transfer to a colander lined with paper towels and gently squeeze out any moisture from the zoodles. Set aside.
In a large microwave safe bowl, combine the mascarpone cheese, parmesan cheese, Romano cheese, salt, pepper, and nutmeg. Microwave on high for 1 minute. Stir. Microwave on high for 30 more seconds.

Remove and whisk together until smooth.
Fold in the pesto and mozzarella cheese until fully incorporated. Add the cooked zoodles and stir until well coated.
Transfer to a 2-quart casserole dish and bake in the oven for 10 minutes or until the cheese is bubbling at the edges. Remove and serve immediately.

Snack:

¼ c walnuts

Day 7

Ketones™ upon rising, mixed in 12 oz. water

30 minutes-1 hour later, Keto Coffee™ mixed in 8-10 oz. water

Optional Breakfast:

Crustless Bacon Quiche

8 pastured eggs
½ can coconut milk
1 bunch scallions
½ lb. properly sourced bacon (heritage, pastured)
8 cherry tomatoes, halved
1 yellow pepper, diced
Sea salt and cracked black pepper

Directions: Chop the bacon up and cook until crispy. Do not drain fat. Chop veggies and add until cooked ¾ the way done. Use whatever veggie you want in whatever (reasonable) quantity you want.
In a separate bowl, beat together eggs and coconut milk. The more you beat the eggs here the fluffier they are going to turn out.
Add the beaten eggs to veggie/bacon mixture and stir consistently until it appears like runny scrambled eggs. The eggs should start clumping together. At this point they are ready to go into muffin pan. Use a jumbo muffin pan to get a good amount of eggy goodness in there. Bake at 350° for 10-14 minutes, or until the eggs don't jiggle when you shake the pan.
Remove and rest on a cooling rack, then chill.

Clean Keto

Lunch:

It Works! Shake™ (Creamy Vanilla or Rich Chocolate)

Add 1 scoop creamer and 1 scoop lemon Ketones™

Snack:

Veggies dipped in almond butter

Dinner:

Keto Teriyaki Beef-on-a-Stick

1 lb. grass-fed beef, cut into strips or cubes
1 tsp sesame oil
1 tsp avocado oil (or other light oil)
2 T gluten free soy sauce (tamari)
2 T unseasoned (sugar free) rice wine vinegar
2 T erythritol granulated sweetener

Directions: Combine the sesame oil, avocado oil, soy sauce, rice wine vinegar, and sweetener in a medium bowl. Add the beef pieces and stir to coat. Marinate for at least one hour or up to 24 hours.
Remove beef from refrigerator 30 minutes before cooking. Preheat the grill if using. Divide the meat into four portions (reserve the marinade) and thread onto four skewers along with optional pieces of green onion.
Grill beef skewers over medium heat for 2-3 minutes per side or until desired doneness is reached. Cook the remaining marinade in the microwave for 2 minutes or in a small saucepan for about 5 minutes until fully cooked.
Pour sauce over skewers before serving with sesame seeds as garnish if desired.

Snack:

1-2 Fat Bombs

Day 8

Ketones™ upon rising, mixed in 12 oz. water

30 minutes-1 hour later, Keto Coffee™ mixed in 8-10 oz. water (add creamer if desired)

Lunch:

It Works! Shake™ (Creamy Vanilla or Rich Chocolate)

Add ½ c blueberries and ½ c unsweetened almond milk if desired

Snack:

Avocado Deviled Eggs

4-6 eggs
1 avocado
¼ tsp sea salt
¼ tsp pepper
¼ tsp garlic
¼ tsp chili powder
¼ tsp cumin
¼ tsp smoked paprika, optional
2 T cilantro

Directions: In a medium pot add eggs and cover with water until fully submerged. Bring to a boil, then remove from heat and cover for 12-13 minutes.
Fill a large bowl with ice water and, using a slotted spoon, gently place eggs in the bowl, allowing eggs to chill for 5 minutes.
Remove outer casing from eggs and slice in half lengthwise, removing the yolk.
Add the yolk, along with the avocado and spices, to a bowl, mixing together until well combined. Add the mixture to the egg halves. Drizzle with lime juice and top with cilantro.

Clean Keto

Dinner:

Summer Confetti Salad (Low Carb and Gluten Free)

3 c cauliflower or cauli/broccoli combo
¼ c scallions, chopped
½ c red bell pepper, finely chopped
⅓ c yellow bell pepper, finely chopped
1 c red cabbage, finely chopped
½ c celery, finely chopped
¼ c fresh basil, julienned

Dressing:

¼ c avocado oil
2 tsp fresh lime juice
2 T apple cider vinegar
1½ T minced fresh ginger
2 T granulated sweetener (I use Swerve)
½ tsp kosher salt

Directions: Combine all of the chopped veggies in a large bowl and toss to combine. Combine the dressing ingredients in a blender or NutriBullet® and blend until emulsified, about 30 seconds.
Pour the dressing over the salad and toss well to coat. Store unused portions in the refrigerator for up to 5 days.

Day 9

Ketones™ upon rising, mixed in 12 oz. water

30 minutes-1 hour later, Keto Coffee™ mixed in 8-10 oz. water

Snack:

¼ c macadamia nuts

Lunch:

Ground Turkey Buddha Bowl Salad

2 tsp avocado or olive oil
1 lb. extra lean, 99% fat free ground turkey
1 tsp garlic powder
1 10-oz. bag H.E.B. shaved brussels sprouts salad
2 tsp Bragg Liquid Aminos
½ c spinach
1 T lemon, juiced
4 T large avocado, diced

Directions: Heat oil in large skillet on medium-high heat. Add ground turkey and, using a wooden spoon or spatula, break into smaller crumbles. Sprinkle with garlic powder then cook until well browned. Add Brussels sprouts and continue to cook several minutes, stirring occasionally. Stir in Bragg Liquid Aminos (or tamari gluten free soy sauce) and lemon juice.
To build Buddha bowls, place ½ c spinach in the bottom of a bowl then top with ¾ c turkey, Brussels sprouts mixture, and top with avocado and serve.

Snack:

1-2 Almond Butter Chocolate Fat Bombs

½ c almond butter
¼ c cacao powder
½ c Swerve
½ c coconut oil

Directions: Mix in a bowl and put in mini cupcake papers or silicon tray. Refrigerate and enjoy!

Clean Keto
Dinner:

Zucchini Pasta with Chicken and Pistachios

2-2½ lbs. zucchini (courgettes)
1 T salt
1 T extra-virgin olive oil
2 cloves garlic
¼ tsp ground cumin
¼ tsp ground black pepper
4 boneless, skinless chicken breasts (150 g/4-6 oz. each)
1 T extra-virgin olive oil or ghee
1 tsp salt
½ tsp ground black pepper
2 scallions
1 T lemon juice
7-10 fresh mint leaves
¼ c shelled pistachios

Directions: Julienne the zucchini with the spiralizer. Place the zoodles in a colander and toss them with the salt until the strands are lightly coated. Set the colander in the sink to drain while you prep the other ingredients.

Pound the chicken to ½-inch thickness between two pieces of plastic wrap with the smooth side of the meat hammer, then slice crosswise into strips. Warm the olive oil in a large, non-stick skillet over medium-high heat, 2-3 minutes. Add the chicken, sprinkle it with the salt and pepper, then toss to coat it in the oil. Spread the chicken in a single layer and let it cook undisturbed, 2-3 minutes. Flip with a spatula, separating the pieces, and cook for an additional 2-3 minutes on the other side. Continue to flip and cook the chicken until it's browned and sizzling on most sides, about 2 minutes more. Transfer the chicken to a plate and cover it loosely with aluminum foil. Thinly slice the scallions, mince the mint leaves, and coarsely chop the pistachios. Add everything to a bowl with the lemon juice, mix with a fork, and place nearby because the next part goes quickly.

Place the olive oil in a small bowl. Peel and crush the garlic, then add it to the bowl with the oil. Add the cumin and pepper to the bowl, mix with a fork, and set it nearby. Rinse the zucchini noodles under running water, drain them well, and squeeze them in a clean dish towel to remove excess water. Return the skillet you used for the chicken to the stove and reheat it over medium-high heat, 2-3 minutes. Place the prepared zucchini noodles in the dry pan and sauté them until

just tender, 2-3 minutes. Push the zoodles to the side of the pan and reduce the heat to medium-low. Add the garlic oil to the pan and cook for 20 seconds, stirring constantly. Push the zucchini noodles into the oil and stir gently until they're coated. Turn off the heat and add the chicken to the zoodles, along with the mint-pistachio mixture. Toss to combine.
To serve, divide the pasta among individual bowls and arm everyone with a big spoon to twirl the strands.

Day 10

Ketones™ upon rising, mixed in 12 oz. water

30 minutes-1 hour later, Keto Coffee™ mixed in 8-10 oz. water

Optional Breakfast:

Keto Sausage Crusted Quiche (Low Carb)

12 oz. raw pork sausage roll
5 slices eggplant, peeled (about ½ inch thick)
10 cherry tomatoes, cut in half
2 T fresh parsley, chopped
6 eggs
2 T heavy whipping cream
2 T grated parmesan cheese
¼ tsp kosher salt
⅛ tsp ground black pepper

Directions: Preheat the oven to 375°.
Press the sausage along the bottom and sides of an 8-inch casserole dish or pie plate. Lay the slices of eggplant across the bottom.
Top with the halved cherry tomatoes and fresh parsley.
Combine the eggs, heavy whipping cream, parmesan cheese, salt and pepper in a medium bowl and whisk until blended.
Gently pour over the ingredients in the pan.
Bake in oven for about 40 minutes or until firm in the center and the sausage is fully cooked.
Serve at any temperature.

Clean Keto

Lunch:

Lemon Pound Cake Shake

1 scoop Creamy Vanilla It Works! Shake™
1 scoop lemon Ketones™
1 scoop Keto Creamer

Snack:

¼ c fresh almond butter

Dinner:

Steak Kebabs in Chimichurri Sauce

1¼ lbs. beef (sirloin or Angus), cut into 1-inch cubes
Fresh ground pepper
1¼ tsp kosher salt
1 large red onion, cut into large chunks
18 cherry tomatoes
6 bamboo skewers, soaked in water for 1 hour

For the Chimichurri Sauce:

2 T parsley, finely chopped (no stems)
2 T chopped cilantro
2 T red onion, finely chopped
1 clove garlic, minced
2 T extra-virgin olive oil
2 T apple cider vinegar
1 T water
¼ tsp kosher salt
⅛ tsp fresh black pepper
⅛ tsp crushed red pepper flakes, or more to taste

Directions: Season the meat with salt and pepper.
For the chimichurri, combine the red onion, vinegar, salt and olive oil and let it sit for about 5 minutes. Add the remaining ingredients and mix; set aside in the refrigerator until ready to use (can be made a few hours ahead).

Place the onions, beef and tomatoes onto the skewers.
Prepare the grill on high heat. Grill the steaks to desired doneness, about 2-3 minutes per side for medium-rare. Transfer steaks to a platter and top with chimichurri sauce.

Snack:

20 olives of choice, or 1-2 fat bombs

Day 11

Ketones™ upon rising, mixed in 12 oz. water

30 minutes-1 hour later, Keto Coffee™ mixed in 8-10 oz. water

Optional Breakfast:

Scrambled Eggs with Homemade Salsa

1 tomato
¼ shallot
1 green onion
¼ jalapeño
½ tsp minced garlic
¼ c chopped cilantro
¼ c lime
3 eggs
1 T olive oil

Directions: Dice tomatoes. Peel and mince shallot. Thinly slice green onion and mince jalapeño pepper. Combine all together in a bowl with garlic and cilantro. Squeeze lime over the top and sprinkle with a pinch of pink sea salt. Toss together to combine. Whisk eggs together in a small bowl. Add oil to skillet and add eggs. Stir regularly until set but moist, about 4 minutes. Top scrambled eggs with fresh salsa.

Snack:

½ c nuts of choice (low carb)

Clean Keto

Lunch:

Tuna Salad with Kalamata Olives and Cherry Tomatoes

2 5-oz. cans wild-caught tuna
½ red onion, chopped
½ c Kalamata olives, pitted
½ c bell peppers, chopped
2 T capers
1 c cherry tomatoes, sliced
⅓ c Paleo/vegan mayo
⅓ c Dijon mustard
½ tsp salt
½ tsp pepper

Toppings:

½ c green onions, chopped
¼ c micro greens

Directions: Add all the ingredients to a large bowl, mixing until well-combined. Keep refrigerated until ready to serve. Top with chopped green onions and micro greens.

Dinner:

It Works! Shake™ (Creamy Vanilla or Rich Chocolate)

So simple on-the-go!

Snack:

Lemon Ketones™ mixed in 12 oz. water

Day 12

Ketones™ upon rising, mixed in 12 oz. water

30 minutes-1 hour later, Keto Coffee™ mixed in 8-10 oz. water (add Keto Creamer if you like)

Optional Breakfast:

Spinach, Mushroom, and Feta Crustless Quiche

14-Day Keto Meal Plan

8 oz. button mushrooms
1 clove garlic, minced
10 oz. box frozen spinach, thawed
4 large eggs
1 c milk
2 oz. feta cheese
¼ c parmesan cheese, grated
½ c shredded mozzarella
Salt and pepper to taste

Directions: Preheat the oven to 350°. Squeeze the excess moisture from the thawed spinach. Rinse any dirt or debris from the mushrooms, slice thinly. Mince the garlic.
Add the mushrooms, garlic, and a pinch of salt and pepper to a non-skillet spritzed lightly with non-stick spray (or a splash of cooking oil). Sauté the mushrooms and garlic until the mushrooms are soft and all of their moisture has evaporated away (5-7 minutes).
Coat a 9-inch pie dish with non-stick spray. Place the squeeze-dried spinach in the bottom of the pie dish. Place the sautéed mushrooms on top of the spinach, followed by the crumbled feta.
In a medium bowl, whisk together the eggs, milk, and parmesan. Season lightly with pepper. Pour the egg mixture over the vegetables and feta in the pie dish. Top with the shredded mozzarella. Place the pie dish on a baking sheet for easy transfer in and out of the oven. Bake the crustless quiche for 45-55 minutes, or until the top is golden brown (ovens may vary). Cut into six slices and serve.

Snack:

20 stuffed olives (stuffed with almonds/feta/blue cheese or peppers)

Clean Keto

Lunch:

Salad of choice with Homemade Ranch Dressing

Dressing:

½ c vegan mayo
1 T fresh dill
½ tsp garlic powder

Directions: Stir and refrigerate.

Snack:

½ c macadamia nuts

Dinner:

Tom Kha Gai Recipe: A Thai Coconut Chicken Soup

3 lemongrass stalks
1 16-oz. can coconut milk
1 T red chili paste
1½ c mushrooms, chopped
½ small lime, juiced
3 boneless, skinless chicken breasts
8 c chicken bone broth
1 inch ginger, chopped
1 red pepper, sliced
½ shallot, sliced into rounds
1 c cilantro, chopped

Directions: Crush the lemongrass stalks. In a large pot over medium-low heat combine broth, lemongrass and ginger, steep for 25 minutes. Remove the ginger and lemongrass bits.
Add chicken, shallots, peppers, mushrooms and chili paste, then bring to a boil. Simmer on low for 20 minutes until chicken is cooked and veggies are soft. Remove from heat and add coconut milk, lime juice and cilantro. Serve warm.

Day 13

Ketones™ upon rising, mixed in 12 oz. water

30 minutes-1 hour later, Keto Coffee™ mixed in 8-10 oz. water (add Keto Creamer and chocolate It Works!™ Greens if you like).

Lunch:

It Works!™ Lemon Pound Cake Shake

Snack:

Avocado Hummus with Veggies

1 15-oz. can no-salt-added chickpeas
1 ripe avocado, halved and pitted
1 c fresh cilantro leaves
¼ c tahini
¼ c extra-virgin olive oil
¼ c lemon juice
1 clove garlic
1 tsp ground cumin
½ tsp salt

Directions: Drain chickpeas, reserving 2 T of the liquid. Transfer the chickpeas and the reserved liquid to a food processor. Add avocado, cilantro, tahini, oil, lemon juice, garlic, cumin and salt. Puree until very smooth. Serve with veggies.

Clean Keto

Dinner:

Cobb Salad Recipe with Avocado Dressing

4 oz. bacon, cooked and chopped
4 oz. smoked salmon, shredded
2 boiled eggs, crescented
¼ c goat cheese crumbles
2 c romaine, chopped
2 c kale, chopped
¼ c chickpeas
2 radishes, julienned
1 green onion, chopped
2 roasted red peppers, finely chopped

Dressing:

1 lime, juiced
¼ c cilantro
½ avocado
1 T avocado oil
1 tsp chipotle powder
1 T goat milk yogurt (optional)
1 jalapeño

Directions: In a food processor, NutriBullet®, or blender, combine dressing ingredients and blend until smooth. Keep the dressing refrigerated until use.
Layer all ingredients evenly between two bowls for serving. Top with dressing and serve.

Snack:

1-2 Lemon Fat bombs

7 oz. coconut butter, softened
¼ c extra-virgin coconut oil, softened
1-2 T organic lemon zest <u>or</u> lemon extract (1-2 tsp), depending on your palate
15-20 drops stevia extract or 1-2 T Swerve
Optional: pinch sea salt or pink Himalayan salt

Day 14

Ketones™ upon rising, mixed in 12 oz. iced water

30 minutes-1 hour later, Keto Coffee™ mixed in 8-12 oz. water (add Keto Creamer and chocolate It Works!™ Greens if you like)

Snack:

¼ c almond butter

Lunch:

Zucchini Basil Pesto Shrimp Salad

2-4 cups fresh shrimp
5-6 medium zucchinis (2¼ -2½ lbs. total), trimmed
¾ tsp salt, divided
1 ripe avocado
1 c packed fresh basil leaves
¼ c unsalted, shelled pistachios
2 T lemon juice
¼ tsp ground pepper
Old Bay seasoning to taste
¼ c extra-virgin olive oil, plus 2 T, divided

Directions: Using a spiral vegetable slicer or a vegetable peeler, cut zucchini lengthwise into long, thin strands or strips. Stop when you reach the seeds in the middle (seeds make the noodles fall apart). Place the zoodles in a colander and toss with ½ tsp salt. Let drain for 15 to 30 minutes, gently squeeze to remove any excess water. Meanwhile, combine avocado, basil, pistachios, lemon juice, pepper and the remaining ¼ tsp salt in a food processor. Pulse until finely chopped. Add ¼ cup oil and process until smooth. Heat 1 T oil in a large skillet over medium-high heat. Add garlic and cook, stirring, for 30 seconds. Add shrimp and sprinkle with Old Bay Seasoning (to taste); cook, stirring occasionally, until the shrimp is almost cooked through, 3-4 minutes. Transfer to a large bowl. Add the remaining 1 T oil to the pan. Add the drained zucchini noodles and gently toss until hot, about 3 minutes. Transfer to the bowl, add the pesto, and gently toss to combine.

Clean Keto

Snack:

20 stuffed olives

Dinner:

Baked Keto Chicken Tenders in Buffalo Sauce with Veggies

1 lb. chicken breast tenders
1 c almond flour
1 large egg
1 T heavy whipping cream
6 oz. buffalo sauce (pre-made). Moore's Original Buffalo Wing Sauce is my favorite.
Salt and pepper
Veggies of choice

Directions: Preheat oven to 350°.
Season chicken tenders with salt and pepper. Season the almond flour generously with salt and pepper. Beat 1 egg together with 1 T of heavy cream.
Dip each tender first in the egg wash and then into the seasoned almond flour. We like to place the tenders in a Tupperware container with the almond flour and shake to coat. A Ziploc bag also works well. Place tenders on a lightly greased baking sheet. Add veggies to baking sheet too. Bake for 30 minutes. If they are not as crispy as you would like you can additionally broil them for 2-3 minutes. Allow tenders to cool for 5 minutes and then place them in a Tupperware container, add the buffalo sauce and shake to coat. Gently shaking is best to prevent the batter from falling off.

Snack:

Lemon Ketones™

APPENDIX

Depending on your health or your sickness, one or more of these supplements or products may help speed you along the path toward perfect health. I know they sure have for me! You can order these It Works™ products from me by calling 812-455-6897, or shopping online at www.staciholweger.com.

SUPPLEMENTS

It Works! Greens™ Superfood: Super yummy berry or chocolate powder packed with 52 nutrient-rich superfoods, fruits, veggies, and herbs to boost your immune system, alkalize your body, and detox daily. Soy free, non-GMO, dairy free, and vegan.

KETOWORKS PRODUCTS

Keto Coffee™: Fuel your body and brain with It Works! Keto Coffee™ powered by KetoWorks™. With grass-fed butter and Medium Chain Triglycerides (MCTs), this instant Keto Coffee™ helps to increase your body's ketone production to rapidly breakdown fat, boost your energy, and sharpen your focus. Medium Chain Triglycerides (MCTs) are one of the healthiest fats! Unlike long chain triglycerides, MCTs do not raise unhealthy cholesterol levels and the calories are not stored in the body as fat. The unique fatty acids of MCT Oil are metabolized more efficiently in your body, converting fat into fuel by increasing ketone production and the process of ketosis. This helps to boost and sustain your energy output, sharpen mental focus, and enhance your mood. The MCT Oil found in It Works! Keto Coffee™ is derived from the finest natural sources—coconut and palm kernel oil. Higher in omega-3 fatty acids, the high-quality fat content helps to fill you up, kill cravings, and satisfy hunger.

Collagen is a protein that when broken down in your body converts to amino acids, which help to build and restore vital protein in your body. Amino acids and protein are crucial for building lean muscle that helps you to burn more calories and fat for fuel! By including collagen peptides, It Works! Keto Coffee™ supports a ketogenic diet of moderate protein, low carbs, and high fat.

KETONES

It Works! Ketones™ is a therapeutic ketone powder with Beta -Hydroxybutyrate (BHB) salts and ketogenic aminos that increase your body's ketone production and the process of ketosis. It helps to keep your body energized in fat-burning mode and to reach peak performance quickly, delivering

Clean Keto

increased energy, endurance and mental focus.

Beta-Hydroxybutyrate (BHB) is a compound that your body makes from fat in the absence of carbohydrate intake. It is used by the body to be converted into ketones. BHB helps your body produce energy in the absence of glucose. Waiting for your body to make the switch from carb metabolism to fat metabolism (the process of ketosis) can be an uncomfortable and lengthy process. It Works! Ketones™ with BHB salts raises the level of ketones in your blood, which means that you have an extra source of energy and will help you get back into ketosis quickly.

Fermented L-leucine, L-isoleucine and L-lysine HCl make up the ketogenic aminos in It Works! Ketones™. Their presence helps your body increase the production of ketones.

COLLAGEN

This beauty-boosting formula contains a blend of advanced collagen proteins and peptides that work together to hydrate, plump, and reveal radiant skin.

It works inside the body to support healthy joints, contribute to healthier looking hair and activate, protect, and improve the appearance of your skin from within!

5 types of collagen blended into one beauty-boosting formula. TruMarine™ Collagen helps to decrease the appearance of wrinkles.

Bioactive collagen peptides trigger fibroblasts to produce Hyaluronic Acid which is critical in providing the bounce and plumpness of skin hydration.

Essential vitamins vital to maintaining youthful, hydrated, and radiant skin!

Vitamins A & C, plus selenium help to slow down the appearance of aging skin by fighting oxidative stress from free radicals.

VEGAN SHAKE

It Works! Shake™ is a clean, plant-based protein powder that will help you energize your workouts, build lean muscle mass, and support your healthy metabolism. With only 100 calories per serving, the It Works! Shake™ provides 15 grams of protein in a proprietary blend of yellow pea and organic sprouted brown rice proteins. This "perfect protein" blend contains a balanced amino acid profile with nine essential amino acids and an optimal concentration of branched-chain amino acids (BCAAs), supporting your optimal health by encouraging lean muscle growth, supporting strength and power during exercise, sustaining your energy, and promoting a faster post-workout recovery! The plant-based protein crushes cravings to help you feel fuller longer.

ACKNOWLEDGMENTS

First and foremost, I would like to thank my mom, Rita Sparks, for providing a perfect example of what it means to eat healthy. She always had a huge garden, or even two, that she tended to all spring and summer long to make sure that she provided the freshest vegetables and fruits for our family. Even though as a child I didn't enjoy those types of foods, she was still modeling that behavior and what the ideal healthy diet should look like. She always prepared fresh, hot breakfasts, made our lunch for school, and had dinner waiting on the table when my dad got home from work. We all sat down as a family and ate together; I was the child that always threw my meat under the table to the eight-pound teacup poodle. Nevertheless, my mom was still there modeling good behavior, good, healthy eating habits, and what it looked like to prepare home-cooked meals.

Over the years she continued to expand on her knowledge of foods and recipes and always made the most amazing home cooked meals. When we would go to my parents' home for birthday dinners, we would get to pick the exact meal that we wanted. I never really cared that much about meat, as I've mentioned, so I always picked something that everybody else would enjoy. Whether it was my dad's teriyaki chicken on the grill, or maybe some fresh fish, my main picks were always the side dishes. I loved my mom's homemade mashed potatoes, and I always enjoyed her mixture of veggies or a great big, healthy salad bar where we could pick all the different things we wanted to put on our bed of romaine lettuce. And, of course, she always made the best desserts ever. Not vegan or keto, ha-ha! But still homemade and super yummy!

Even as I write this, I'm extremely emotional. Food has never been something that triggered an emotion for me but writing this brings back so many memories, and I'm so grateful that I had such a wonderful role model in my mom to show me what good, healthy cooking looks like.

Next, I would like to thank my husband of 20+ years, Brent.

All throughout our marriage he has been extremely supportive of all the different endeavors that I've chosen, and this one isn't any different. If anything, he's encouraged me to do this even when I doubted I could. I have never thought of myself as a writer or someone who would create books. I read all the time, I have lots and lots of information floating around in my brain, and I love to share it with people verbally. I love to teach, but I've never thought of using writing as a platform to get my messages across. Brent happened to meet a professional book editor and publisher, connected her with me, and my journey began. I want to acknowledge Barbara Dee and the team at Suncoast Digital Press for helping me bring this labor of love into to the world.

Thank you, Brent, for encouraging me to step out of my comfort zone on this one, and to do things that push me beyond what I would normally do. Your support means the world to me, not just for me but for our family, our children. You're always there and I am forever grateful that you stay by my side through all my endeavors. I love you!

I would also like to thank the many people that asked me over the last three years where my cookbook was and for letting me know they would buy it as soon as it was available, even though I didn't think there would ever be one available! Whether it was online through my social media sites, in person at the gym, or at different events, people were asking me for my recipes because they were watching what I was doing. I'm forever grateful for these people who continually planted the seed. They wanted what I had and it would benefit them to have it. I'm so grateful that they felt prompted to share this with me all these years and to build my belief and confidence that I could actually do something like this and it would be worthwhile. So, thank you for being so vocal and letting me know that there was a need for this in the marketplace.

ACKNOWLEDGMENTS

If you would've told me over three years ago when I was enjoying my cheese and crackers for dinner each night that someday I would be an author of a vegan cookbook, I would've told you that you had lost your mind. This book never would've been written if it weren't for my daughter planting that seed in my mind all those years ago. Taylor has always been my inspiration for learning and growing. She is such a blessing in more ways than I could ever express.

I would like to thank my good friend, Carla Burns, for opening up her beautiful kitchen for the photo shoot on the front cover. It is absolutely stunning and it fits in perfectly with the feeling of a Clean Keto lifestyle.

Thank you to my photographer, Sean Malley, who made this process effortless for me. I am not one that likes to be photographed and Sean's level of professionalism and perfection in a "flash" made shooting this front cover simple and fun.

The talented Jessica Marie got me camera-ready, and I am grateful for not only the simple make-up tips I learned from her in the session, but also for the relationship that started to form that day. You just never know who God will put in your path and for what reason. Jess shared with me a very exciting therapy option for Taylor that I had never heard of that has been working for her precious daughter. You never know where your blessings are going to come from! Jess, many blessings to you and your baby girl.

I want to thank my amazing circle of friends from the bottom of my heart. You have supported me through this whole process and encouraged me to be the best version of myself. Your feedback on this journey has been priceless. I appreciate your honesty and openness with me each time I asked a question. God brings some people into your life for a reason, some for a season, and some for a lifetime…you are my lifetime friends, who will forever be family to me. Love you all dearly!

And last but certainly not least, I have the deepest appreciation for Dream Oaks Camp. This camp for special needs children in Bradenton, Florida, has dramatically changed my daughter's life. Our family is forever grateful for everything you have done for her and will continue to do in the future. She loves and adores each and every one of the staff members and now has a group of friends

Clean Keto

who love her for who she really is, on the inside, no matter what the outside looks like. You at Dream Oaks Camp have all pulled out the best in Taylor and shown her that she matters and that you love her more than words can describe. This is why I am so happy to be able to donate ALL proceeds from the sales of this cookbook to the camp, specifically for the purpose of providing scholarships to the many other special needs children that DESERVE the same monthly or summer program opportunities. All children deserve to feel wanted and special—Dream Oaks is a place that accomplishes just that and I am ready to help put them on the map! Let's all help more kids feel amazing about themselves.

"History will judge us by the difference we make in the everyday lives of children."

—Nelson Mandela

ABOUT THE AUTHOR

Staci Holweger is an entrepreneur and leadership coach, a holistic health practitioner, and a former cheese addict who once muttered the words, "I would never be a vegan." She found her passion for food traveling the world and experiencing different recipes.

Staci comes from a background in teaching English and is currently getting her PhD in integrative medicine. She has been coaching people from all over the country on eating a vegan/keto lifestyle for over three years now and she has an active social media presence with over 15,000 followers.

Staci lives in Sarasota, Florida, with her family, and when she is not cooking, she loves reading, working out, and traveling.

Staci's web site: www.staciholweger.com

Made in the USA
Middletown, DE
05 January 2020